MINI FLAGS ATLAS OF THE WORLD

Published by AND Cartographic Publishers Ltd
Alberto House, Hogwood Lane
Finchampstead, Berks, RG40 4RF
United Kingdom
email: info@andmap.com

First edition 1999
Copyright © 1999 AND Cartographic Publishers Ltd

ISBN 0-9533246-3-X

987654321

Copy editor: Helen King
Designer: Phil Jacobs
Photo research: Jenny Speller
Cover design: Richard Fox

Photographs:
All pictures sourced from Corbis Images unless credited below:
Mary Evans Picture Library *p8 both;*
Phil Jacobs *pp 46,64,81,116, 223, 231.*
Stamps provided by Stanley Gibbons, except *pp: 86, 203, 216.*

Note:
the red dots on the maps
indicate capital cities

Flags:
Authenticated by The Flag Institute, UK and
The Flag Research Center, USA.

Originated by JobColor srl, Bergamo, Italy

Printed by Editoriale Lloyd srl, Trieste, Italy

MINI
Flags Atlas
OF THE
WORLD

Pat Jacobs

Contents

Contents

Parts and types of flags

The hoist is generally the third of the flag closest to the staff

Upper hoist

A specialised vocabulary
has developed to describe
the patterns and parts of a flag.
   It is assumed that the flag is
flying from a staff on the right.
The side facing the observer is called
the obverse and the other side is the
reverse. These are normally identical, the
exceptions being the flag of Paraguay, certain
state flags and those bearing inscriptions, which
must read correctly on both sides.

Lower hoist

Types of flag
The most common flag patterns are
stripes or other geometric designs, easily
recognisable from a distance.

Cross

Scandinavian cross

Saltire

Coupled or Greek cross

Canton

Swallow-tail

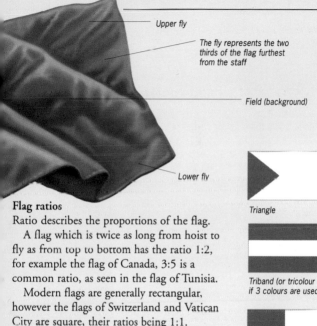

Upper fly

The fly represents the two
thirds of the flag furthest
from the staff

Field (background)

Lower fly

Triangle

Triband (or tricolour
if 3 colours are used)

Bicolour

Flag ratios

Ratio describes the proportions of the flag.

A flag which is twice as long from hoist to
fly as from top to bottom has the ratio 1:2,
for example the flag of Canada, 3:5 is a
common ratio, as seen in the flag of Tunisia.

Modern flags are generally rectangular,
however the flags of Switzerland and Vatican
City are square, their ratios being 1:1.

Some flags are distinguished by their
unusual proportions, such as the flag of Qatar
which has the ratio 11:28.

Serration

Pennant

Fimbriation

How modern flags began

The first flags were created around 3,000 BC when the Chinese attached pieces of silk to poles. Early banners marked rallying points on the battlefield and often bore religious symbols, such as the Christian cross or Islamic crescent, which are still in use today.

Forerunners of modern flags included Roman vexilloids – staffs with emblems attached.

The 16th, 17th and 18th centuries saw the creation of several flags born of the revolutionary struggle, which were an inspiration for flags around the world.

The *Prinsenvlag*

Conceived in the late 16th century, during the Dutch War of Rebellion against Spanish domination, the horizontal tricolour of the Netherlands was the first revolutionary flag. When Peter the Great of Russia visited the country in the late 1690s he was inspired to adopt a similar tricolour. This, in turn, determined flag design throughout Eastern Europe.

The flag of the Netherlands was called the Prinsenvlag *after Prince William of Orange, who led the Dutch fight for liberty.*

The Stars and Stripes

The most famous and widely copied flag in the world, the Stars and Stripes, was created during the revolutionary war of 1775-83 when 13 British colonies rebelled against the mother country.

The Anarchist Flag

Like the red flag on which it was based, the diagonal red and black Anarchist bicolour was first used during the French Revolution. The colours are said to represent 'freedom or death' and have survived in the flag of Angola and the former flag of Haiti, as well as in the banners of numerous revolutionary groups.

The French *Tricolore*

The French Revolution also gave birth to the *tricolore*. The storming of the Bastille in 1789 led to the ousting of the Bourbon monarchy and the creation of a flag combining red and blue (the colours of Paris) with white, which represented the Bourbons.

The tricolore, *created during the Revolution of 1789, became a symbol of liberty and a model for many other national flags. This poster invites Parisians to join the Revolution of 1848.*

Canada

White stands for snow

The maple leaf is a traditional Canadian emblem

Red recalls Canadian lives lost during World War I

Flag ratio: 1:2

Effective date: 15 February 1965

Use: National and civil

Area: 9,975,000 sq. km (3,850,350 sq. miles)

Capital: Ottawa

Population: 29,600,000

Main languages: English, French

Principal religions: Roman Catholic, Protestant

Currency: Canadian dollar

Until 1965 Canada flew the British Red Ensign with the Canadian arms in the fly. Prime Minister Lester Pearson felt that this no longer reflected the increasingly multi-ethnic nation so, amid much opposition, a new flag was sought.

The initial design, known as 'Pearson's Pennant', bore green maple leaves with blue bars on either side to represent the Atlantic and Pacific oceans. While the use of a maple leaf was agreed, it was decided that the flag should be red and white, the national colours since 1921.

A French memorial to Canadians killed during the Battles of Arras.

Canada – Provincial flags

Provinces are listed according to the dates
they joined the Confederation.

 New
Brunswick
1867

*The province is named after the
British royal family of Brunswick-
Lüneburg (Hannover) and its links
with Britain are represented by the
lion. The heraldic ship recalls New
Brunswick's ship-building industry.*

 Nova Scotia
1867

*The flag reflects the province's name
which is Latin for New Scotland.
Based on the provincial arms, it
consists of a blue St Andrew's cross on
a white field with the Royal Arms of
Scotland in the centre.*

 Ontario
1867

*This flag is similar to the Red Ensign
previously flown by Canada and was
the first to use the maple leaf. It bears
the shield from the arms of Ontario
which depicts a sprig of maple leaves
below a St George's cross.*

 Québec
1867

*The most widely-used provincial
flag is the Fleurdelysé of French-
speaking Québec. It is based on the
fleur-de-lys emblem commonly used
in France and also bears a white
cross of St George.*

 Manitoba
1870

*The flag recalls the former British
Red Ensign of Canada. The shield
from the provincial arms, which
appears in the fly, bears an image of
buffalo standing on rock below the
cross of St George.*

 Northwest
Territories
1870

*Blue represents the Territories' lakes
and rivers while white stands for
snow. The shield depicts the polar ice
below which are an Arctic fox and
gold bars, symbolising the region's
forests and mineral resources.*

Canada – Provincial flags

 British Columbia 1871

Based on the province's arms, the flag depicts the setting sun against the sea and illustrates the motto, 'Splendour that Never Sets'.

 Prince Edward Island 1873

The provincial flag, derived from the arms, shows an oak tree and three saplings below an elongated version of the British lion.

 Yukon Territory 1898

The flag's colours symbolise the forests, snow and lakes. The arms represent the mountains, rich in minerals, the English pioneers and the fur trade.

 Alberta 1905

The shield depicts the wheat fields which dominate the province, while the cross of St George recalls Alberta's historical links with England.

 Saskatchewan 1905

Yellow represents the wheat fields of 'Canada's Breadbasket', while green recalls the northern forests. The prairie lily is the provincial emblem.

 Newfoundland and Labrador 1949

White stands for snow and ice, blue for the sea, red for human endeavour and gold for confidence in the future. The design recalls the Union Jack.

 Newfoundland Island

The tricolour dates from 1843 and reflects the origins of the early settlers: pink stands for England, white for Scotland and green for Ireland.

 Labrador

The flag of the Labrador peninsula symbolises the region's snows, forests and waters. The spruce twig represents the territory's three races.

United States of America

White signifies purity and innocence

Red stands for hardiness and valour

Blue represents vigilance, perseverance and justice

The latest star, representing Hawaii, was added in 1960.

Flag ratio: 10:19
Effective date:
4 July 1960

Use: National and civil

Area:
9,363,520 sq. km
(3,615,276 sq. miles)

Capital:
Washington DC

Population:
263,000,000

Main languages:
English, Spanish

Principal religions:
Protestant,
Roman Catholic

Currency: US dollar

Englishman navigator, John Cabot, reached North America in 1497 and, on the basis of this voyage, England claimed the entire continent. Protesting against taxes levied by the British, 13 colonies declared independence on 4 July 1776.

The first Stars and Stripes, which originated in 1777, bore 13 stripes and 13 stars, representing the rebel colonies.

In 1818 Congress decreed that a star would be added on the 4th of July following the admission of each new state. To date, there have been 27 versions as new states have been added.

Buzz Aldrin salutes the Stars and Stripes, hoisted on the moon following the Apollo 11 landing in 1969.

USA – Historical flags

The forerunner of the Stars and Stripes was the Grand Union Flag, introduced in December 1775. It had 13 alternating red and white stripes symbolising unity between the 13 colonies which rebelled against the British however, since the prevailing hope was for reconciliation, the Union Jack appeared in the canton.

The Stars and Stripes was created when, in 1777, Congress decreed that '…the Union be 13 stars white in a blue field representing a new constellation.' When Vermont and Kentucky were admitted in 1795 two further stars and stripes were incorporated. Anticipating the effect of future additions, it was decided in 1818 to restrict the stripes to 13, while increasing the number of stars.

The Stars and Bars

The American Civil War, 1861-65, arose out of a dispute concerning the continued existence of slavery in the Southern States. Eleven states elected to leave the Union and established the Confederate Government which adopted its own flag, known as the Stars and Bars.

The Battle Flag

A more distinctive flag was needed for use on the battlefield, so in 1861 the Battle Flag, or Southern Cross, was born.

Stars rarely appeared on flags before the introduction of the Stars and Stripes.

USA – State flags

States are listed according to the dates they joined the Union.

 Delaware 1787

Delaware was first to join the Union in 1787, a date recalled by its flag. The colours are based on uniforms worn in the War of Independence.

 Pennsylvania 1787

The arms depict a plough, three wheatsheaves and a sailing ship. A scroll below bears the state motto 'Virtue, Liberty and Independence'.

 New Jersey 1787

The buff colour is derived from uniforms worn during the War of Independence. The arms illustrate the motto 'Liberty and Prosperity'.

 Georgia 1787

The state seal symbolises the three branches of government. In 1956 the flag was redesigned to include the Southern Cross in the fly.

 Connecticut 1788

The flag recalls a standard used during the Civil War. The three vines in the arms symbolise the colonies which united to form the state.

 Massachusetts 1788

Until 1971 the flag bore the arms on the obverse and a pine tree on the reverse. Both sides now show the arms, depicting an Amerindian.

 Maryland 1788

This flag is the heraldic banner of Lord Baltimore, founder of the colony, and is based on the arms of his parents' families.

 South Carolina 1788

The flag is based on that of American Revolutionary general William Moultrie. The palmetto tree in the centre is a state emblem.

USA – State flags

 New Hampshire
1788

The state seal depicts the frigate Raleigh while the nine stars indicate that New Hampshire was the ninth state to join the Union.

 Virginia
1788

The seal shows a triumphant female figure trampling on a fallen man. Below is the Latin motto, Sic Semper Tyrannis (Thus always to tyrants).

 New York
1788

The flag, which originally had a buff field, is based on that used during the War of Independence. The shield shows two ships on the Hudson River.

 North Carolina
1789

The design of this flag is reminiscent of the Stars and Bars. The emblem includes scrolls showing important dates in the state's history.

 Rhode Island
1790

An anchor, symbolising hope, appears within a ring of stars representing the first states to enter the Union, of which Rhode Island was 13th.

 District of Columbia
1791

This territory (not a state) includes the capital, Washington, named after the first president. The flag is derived from the Washington family arms.

 Vermont
1795

The arms of Vermont depict a pine tree, a cow and three wheatsheaves. The scroll bears the state's name and the motto, 'Freedom and unity'.

 Kentucky
1795

The motto, 'United we stand, divided we fall', is illustrated in the seal which shows two men shaking hands. Below are two stems of goldenrod.

USA – State flags

Tennessee
1818

The flag recalls the Battle Flag of the Civil War. The stars indicate that Tennessee was the third state to join the Union after the original 13.

Ohio
1818

The 'O' in the hoist stands for Ohio and the stars indicate that the state was the 17th to join the Union. The flag's distinctive shape is unique.

Louisiana
1818

The pelican, a state emblem, is shown pecking at herself to feed her young symbolising self-sacrifice. The scroll reads, 'Union, Justice & Confidence.'

Indiana
1818

The circles of stars stand for the states which joined the Union before Indiana – represented by the large star. The torch is a symbol of liberty.

Mississippi
1818

The flag is adapted from the Stars and Bars while the Battle Flag appears in the canton. The colours recall the French tricolore.

Illinois
1819

The emblem, taken from the state seal, depicts an eagle holding a red scroll bearing the state motto, 'State Sovereignty, National Union'.

Alabama
1820

Alabama became a founding member of the Confederate States during the Civil War and its square flag recalls the Battle Flag.

Maine
1820

Maine is known as The Pine Tree State and a pine tree appears in the arms. Above is the North Star and the motto, 'Dirigo' (I direct).

USA – State flags

 Missouri
1822

The stars signify that the state was the 24th to join the Union. The flag's colours recall French Louisiana, of which Missouri was a part.

 Arkansas
1836

The upper star represents the Confederate States. The lower three stand for countries which have ruled the state: Spain, France and the US.

 Michigan
1837

The flag bears a Latin motto, meaning 'If you seek a pleasant peninsula, look about you', referring to Michigan's two large peninsulas.

 Florida
1845

The seal shows an Indian woman scattering flowers. The red saltire was added in 1900, recalling the Battle Flag used during the Civil War.

 Texas
1846

Texas was named the Lone Star State after the single star on its flag, first adopted by the independent Republic of Texas in 1839.

 Iowa
1847

Once part of French Louisiana, Iowa's flag recalls the tricolore. The scroll reads 'Our liberties we prize and our rights we will maintain'.

 Wisconsin
1848

Wisconsin's nickname, The Badger State, refers to the miners who burrowed in search of lead. The state seal recalls mining and seafaring.

 California
1851

Once part of Mexico, the break-away California Republic adopted this flag in 1846. The star and stripe express the republic's desire to join the Union.

USA – State flags

Minnesota
1858

The 19 stars within the white circle signify that Minnesota, represented by the top star, was the 19th state to join the Union after the original 13.

Oregon
1859

The only state flag with a different design on each side. The obverse bears the arms encircled by 33 stars. On the reverse a beaver recalls fur trading.

Kansas
1861

The seal depicts agriculture and bears the motto, 'Ad Astra per Aspera' (To the stars through difficulties). Above is the state emblem, a sunflower.

West Virginia
1863

The motto translates as 'Mountaineers are always free'. The arms show a farmer and a miner within a wreath of rhododendron, the state flower.

Nevada
1865

The motto, 'Battle Born', recalls the state's admission to the Union during the Civil War. A wreath of sagebrush, the state flower, surrounds the star.

Nebraska
1867

The state seal features a blacksmith at work on the banks of the Missouri River. The motto shown on the scroll reads, 'Equality before the law'.

Colorado
1876

Blue and white represent the blue skies and snow-covered mountains. Red and yellow were the colours of the Spanish who first explored the area.

Idaho
1890

Based on the military colours, the flag bears Idaho's seal, showing a woman holding a spear and scales, a miner and a mountainous landscape.

USA – State flags

Montana
1889

Montana's mountainous terrain is depicted in the seal and its mineral wealth is reflected by the state motto, 'Oro y Plata' (Gold and silver).

North Dakota
1889

The flag, adopted in 1911, dates back to the Spanish-American War of 1898 and is based on the colours of the First North Dakota Infantry.

South Dakota
1889

The flag had different designs on the obverse and the reverse until 1963, when it was revised to show the state seal on both sides.

Washington
1889

Known as The Evergreen State, Washington is the only state to fly a green flag. The seal bears a portrait of George Washington.

Wyoming
1890

The flag recalls the herds of bison which once roamed the plains and is based on a design resulting from a competition held in 1916.

Utah
1896

Utah is known as The Beehive State and a beehive appears in the seal on the flag. The year 1847 recalls the founding of the state by the Mormons.

Oklahoma
1907

The winning entry in a competition, the flag symbolises peace between the white settlers and Oklahoma's many Amerindian groups.

Arizona
1912

This flag combines red and yellow, representing Arizona's former Spanish rulers, with the state colours. The copper star stands for mineral wealth.

USA – State and overseas territory flags

 New Mexico
1912

Once ruled by Spain, the state has adopted a flag in the Spanish colours. The emblem is an ancient sun symbol of the Zia Pueblo Indians.

 Alaska
1959

Designed by a 13-year-old boy, the flag shows the Pole Star and the Plough constellation in gold, a colour which reflects Alaska's mineral wealth.

 Hawaii
1959

The stripes of the flag represent the eight main islands. The Union Jack recalls a flag presented to the king in 1793 by explorer, George Vancouver.

 American Samoa

The emblem shows an American eagle holding a Samoan chief's staff and a ceremonial knife, symbolising the protection of Samoa by the US.

 Guam

The flag of Guam can only be flown with the Stars and Stripes. The territory's seal depicts a beach, a coconut palm and a canoe.

 Northern Mariana Islands

The flag is said to symbolise the islands and the Pacific Ocean. Behind the star is a grey Latte stone representing the original inhabitants.

 Puerto Rico

The flag is reminiscent of that of Cuba and dates back to 1895 when both colonies were fighting for independence from Spain.

 Virgin Islands

The emblem is based on the arms of the United States. The eagle holds three arrows, representing the main islands, and an olive branch.

Mexico

The emblem was added to distinguish the flag from that of Italy

The colours are those of the Mexican liberation army

The design is based on the French tricolore

The design of the Mexican flag was inspired by liberal political ideas from Europe – particularly France following the Revolution of 1789.

The coat of arms in the centre is based on an Aztec legend which claimed that a great civilisation would be established in a marshy area where a cactus grew out of a rock. Perched on the cactus, an eagle would be seen eating a snake.

Aztec priests supposedly saw this scene in 1325 when they arrived at the place which was to become the Aztec capital Tenochtitlán, site of present-day Mexico City.

C AMERICA

Flag ratio: 4:7
Effective date: 23 November 1968

Use: National and civil

Area: 1,958,201 sq. km (756,063 sq. miles)

Capital: Mexico City

Population: 90,500,000

Main language: Spanish

Principal religion: Roman Catholic

Currency: Peso

The ancient Aztec legend illustrated in the arms of Mexico.

Guatemala

The quetzal symbolises freedom

The weapons represent the defence of liberty

The blue bands stand for the Caribbean Sea and the Pacific Ocean

Flag ratio: 5:8
Effective date:
15 September 1968
Use: National and state

Area: 108,889 sq. km
(42,042 sq. miles)

Capital:
Guatemala City

Population:
10,600,000

Main languages:
Spanish,
Mayan languages

Principal religion:
Christian

Currency: Quetzal

After three centuries of Spanish rule, followed by two years as part of the Mexican Empire, Guatemala proclaimed independence in 1823 and joined the Central American Federation.

The nation used the blue and white horizontal tricolour of the Federation until 1851 when red and yellow stripes were added, reflecting pro-Spanish sentiments. In 1871 Guatemala reverted to the blue and white flag with the bands arranged vertically.

The country is particularly rich in birdlife and the brilliantly-plumaged quetzal features on the national arms, which appear in the centre. The bird is perched on a scroll showing the date of the Declaration of Independence.

The quetzal is the national bird of Guatemala.

Belize

Blue is the colour of the People's United Party

Sub umbra floreo, 'I flourish in the shade', is the national motto

Flag ratio: 3:5

Effective date: late 1980s

Use: National and civil

Area: 22,696 sq. km (8,763 sq. miles)

Capital: Belmopan

Population: 217,000

Main languages: English, Spanish, Creole

Principal religions: Roman Catholic, Protestant

Currency: Belize dollar

Belize, formerly the colony of British Honduras, gained independence in 1981. The country's flag is based on that of the People's United Party, which began the fight for liberation in 1950, a date recalled by the wreath of 50 leaves. On independence, two red stripes were added to the flag to represent the rival United Democratic Party.

The coat of arms is based on the logging industry. The shield shows a sailing ship transporting timber, above which is an oar and a hammer on the left and a saw and a felling axe on the right.

Like the coat of arms this stamp bears a mahogany tree reflecting the importance of timber to Belize's economy.

24

El Salvador

The triangle represents equality and the rainbow signifies peace

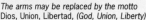

The arms may be replaced by the motto Dios, Union, Libertad, (God, Union, Liberty)

C AMERICA

Flag ratio: 12:21

Effective date: September 1972

Use: National and state

Area: 21,041 sq. km (8,124 sq. miles)

Capital: San Salvador

Population: 5,800,000

Main languages: Spanish, indigenous languages

Principal religion: Roman Catholic

Currency: El Salvador colón

Soon after gaining independence from Spain in 1821, El Salvador came under the domination of the Mexican Empire. When the Empire dissolved the country joined the Central American Federation (CAF), becoming independent in 1841.

El Salvador used the blue and white flag of Central America until 1865, then adopted a design based on the Stars and Stripes. The blue and white triband was restored in 1912.

The five volcanos depicted in the arms recall the original provinces of the CAF as well as the numerous volcanos of Central America, such as Santa Ana shown here.

Honduras

The blue and white triband is based on the flag of the CAF

The stars represent the Federation's five original members

Flag ratio: 1:2

Effective date: 18 January 1949

Use: National and civil

Area: 112,088 sq. km (43,277 sq. miles)

Capital: Tegucigalpa

Population: 5,900,000

Main languages: Spanish, English, indigenous languages

Principal religion: Roman Catholic

Currency: Lempira

Formerly under Spanish rule, Honduras declared independence in 1821, only to be incorporated into the Mexican Empire. The country regained independence in 1823 and joined the Central American Federation (CAF), adopting the association's blue and white flag. On the disintegration of the Federation in 1838 Honduras again declared independence, retaining the triband.

In 1866 five stars were added to represent the former members of the CAF and to express hope for its rebirth.

Francisco Morazán, Honduran-born president of the CAF and champion of Central American federalism.

Nicaragua

The volcanos recall the five nations of the CAF

The triangle signifies equality

Flag ratio: 3:5

Effective date:
27 August 1971

Use: National and civil

Area: 130,000 sq. km
(50,193 sq. miles)

Capital: Managua

Population: 4,500,000

Main languages:
Spanish, English

Principal religion:
Roman Catholic

Currency: Córdoba

After gaining independence from Spain in 1821, Nicaragua became part of the Mexican Empire. In 1823 the country joined the Central American Federation, finally becoming an independent republic in 1838.

In 1908 Nicaragua adopted the blue-white-blue flag common to all the Central American states.

The flag can be used with the emblem, which shares many features with that of El Salvador, or as a plain triband.

The emblem comprises a triangle framing five volcanos, the Cap of Liberty and a rainbow, which symbolises peace.

Costa Rica

Red was added to the blue and white flag to reflect the French tricolore

The sun of freedom rises from the Caribbean Sea

The stars represent Costa Rica's seven provinces

Flag ratio: 3:5

Effective date:
29 September 1848

Use: National and state

Area: 51,100 sq. km
(19,730 sq. miles)

Capital: San José

Population: 3,400,000

Main language: Spanish

Principal religion:
Roman Catholic

Currency:
Costa Rican colón

L ike Guatemala, El Salvador, Honduras and Nicaragua, Costa Rica was ruled by Spain and Mexico before joining the Central American Federation (CAF) in 1821. After the CAF disbanded Costa Rica retained the Federation's blue and white triband.

In 1848 a red band was added in the centre, commemorating the French Revolution which ousted King Louis Philippe, and in 1906 the current pattern was adopted with the coat of arms set towards the hoist.

The Arenal volcano in Costa Rica last erupted in 1968. The flag's emblem depicts three volcanos on the isthmus between the Pacific Ocean and the Caribbean.

Panama

The blue star signifies the purity and honesty of the life of the country

The red star represents authority and law

Flag ratio: 2:3

Effective date:
4 June 1904

Use: National and civil

Area: 75,517 sq. km
(29,157 sq. miles)

Capital: Panama City

Population: 2,600,000

Main languages:
Spanish, English

Principal religion:
Roman Catholic

Currency: Balboa

Previously ruled by Spain, Panama became a province of Columbia in 1821. Following a series of revolts, independence was achieved in 1903 with the support of the United States.

The colours of the country's flag may have been chosen in honour of its US defenders, however blue and red also represented the rival Conservative and Liberal parties, and white stands for peace. The equal standing given to both colours is said to express the wish that the parties should govern in turn, against a background of peace.

This American postage stamp commemorates the 25th anniversary of the Panama Canal, built on a strip of land leased to the US in exchange for a guarantee to protect Panama's independence.

Jamaica

Black, yellow and green are colours found in many African flags and reflect the islanders' heritage

Flag ratio: 1:2
Effective date:
6 August 1962

Use: National and civil

Area: 10,990 sq. km
(4,243 sq. miles)

Capital: Kingston

Population: 2,500,000

Main languages:
English,
English Creole

Principal religions:
Christian, others

Currency:
Jamaican dollar

Jamaica was ruled by Spain until seized by Britain in 1655. The population is primarily of African origin, descended from slaves brought to the island between the 17th and 19th centuries. The country won independence in 1962 and introduced a flag adapted from a design submitted in a national competition.

The colours can be interpreted as symbolising the nation's hopes for the future in spite of hardships, past and present. The diagonal yellow cross stands for sunshine and natural resources. The black triangles recall past burdens – notably slavery – and green represents agriculture and expresses hope for the future.

Agriculture plays an important part in the Jamaican economy and is symbolised by the flag's green triangles.

30

Cuba

The flag is known as the 'Lone Star' banner

The red triangle symbolised the blood shed in the fight for freedom from Spain

The blue stripes stand for Cuba's three provinces

C AMERICA

Flag ratio: 1:2
Effective date: 20 May 1902
Use: National and civil

Area: 110,861 sq. km (42,804 sq. miles)
Capital: Havana
Population: 11,100,000
Main language: Spanish
Principal religion: Roman Catholic
Currency: Cuban peso

A Spanish colony until 1898, Cuba was ruled by an American military government between 1898 and 1902.

The Cuban flag, designed by Venezuelan-born Narciso López, was first used in 1849 by the liberation movement seeking to free Cuba from Spanish rule. López anticipated that the island would become an American state, so the single star, *la Estrella Solitaria*, was intended to join the others on the US flag.

The sign reads 'Matanzas, cradle of the Bay of Pigs' above a mural of communist leader, Fidel Castro. Ironically, in view of his hostility to the United States, the flag is modelled on the Stars and Stripes.

The Bahamas

Blue represents the Caribbean Sea

Yellow stands for the golden beaches

C AMERICA

Flag ratio: 1:2
Effective date:
10 July 1973
Use: National

Area: 13,878 sq. km
(5,358 sq. miles)
Capital: Nassau
Population: 278,000
Main language: English
Principal religions:
Protestant,
Roman Catholic
Currency:
Bahamian dollar

The Bahamas became a British colony in 1783 and full independence was attained in 1973.

When a pre-independence contest to find a new national flag failed to produce a suitable entry, a design was created based on ideas arising from the competition.

The colours reflect the aquamarine seas surrounding the islands' golden beaches and the black triangle in the hoist symbolises the people's unity and resolve.

The flag's blue and yellow bands emphasise the importance of tourism in the islands' economy.

Haiti

Blue represents the black population and links with Africa

Red stands for those of mixed race

The original blue and red flag was based on the French tricolore

Flag ratio: 3:5

Effective date: 25 February 1986

Use: National and civil

Area: 27,750 sq. km (10,714 sq. miles)

Capital: Port-au-Prince

Population: 7,180,000

Main languages: French, French Creole

Principal religions: Roman Catholic, Voodoo

Currency: Gourde

Formerly a French colony, Haiti won independence in 1804 following a rebellion led by former slave, Toussaint L'Ouverture. The country had already adopted a blue and red vertical bicolour and on independence the bands became horizontal.

In 1806 the blue stripe was changed to black, however the blue and red flag was reinstated in western Haiti, bearing the arms and the cap of liberty.

Brutal dictator Papa Doc Duvalier, elected in 1964, adopted the black and red flag, including the arms without the cap of liberty. In 1986, after the fall of his successor, Baby Doc, the blue and red bicolour and the cap of liberty were restored.

The weapons shown on the arms express the Haitians' willingness to defend their freedom.

Dominican Republic

The arms appear on national and state flags

The white cross symbolises faith

The arms show a Bible open at the Gospel of St John, a Trinitarian symbol

Flag ratio: 5:8

Effective date: 14 September 1863

Use: National and state

Area: 48,734 sq. km (18,816 sq. miles)

Capital: Santo Domingo

Population: 7,915,000

Main language: Spanish

Principal religion: Roman Catholic

Currency: Dominican Republic peso

A former Spanish colony, the Dominican Republic was ceded to France in 1795 then annexed to neighbouring Haiti in 1822.

After centuries of foreign rule, the Trinitarian movement was formed to fight for independence. The Trinitarian flag of superimposed a white cross and ten white stars over the blue and red bicolour of Haiti.

In 1844, when the country was liberated, this flag was adopted. The stars were removed and the blue and red quarters in the fly were later reversed to form the present pattern.

The island was discovered by Colombus in 1492 and became the site of the first Spanish settlement in the New World. His remains are said to lie in the cathedral of Santa Domingo.

St Kitts and Nevis

Green represents fertility

Red symbolises the struggle for liberty

Yellow stands for sunshine

Black recalls the people's African origins

Flag ratio: 2:3

Effective date: 19 September 1983

Use: National and civil

Area: 261 sq. km (101 sq. miles)

Capital: Basseterre

Population: 41,000

Main language: English

Principal religions: Protestant, Roman Catholic

Currency: East Caribbean dollar

St Kitts, Nevis and Anguilla were united as a British dependency in 1871, becoming a self-governing member of the West Indies Associated States in 1967. Anguilla withdrew in 1980 and three years later St Kitts and Nevis jointly attained full independence.

A competition was held to design a new flag and the winning entry was created by student, Edrice Lewis. While the stars might be assumed to represent the two islands, in fact they signify hope and freedom.

Nevis has its own distinctive flag depicting Nevis Peak, a mountain at the centre of the island.

Antigua and Barbuda

Black reflects the African origins of the islanders

Red stands for the vigour of the people

White represents hope

Flag ratio: 2:3
Effective date:
27 February 1967
Use: National and civil

Area: 442 sq. km
(171 sq. miles)
Capital: St John's
Population: 66,000
Main language: English
Principal religion:
Protestant
Currency:
East Caribbean dollar

The British colonies of Antigua and Barbuda became a self-governing state in 1967 and a competition was held to create a new flag.

This striking design was chosen from 600 entries. As well as recalling the tourist attractions of fine beaches, blue sea and sunshine, the flag symbolises the islands' heritage and hopes for the future, while the sun illustrates the dawning of a new era.

The flag was retained when the islands attained independence in 1981.

The Admiral's House at English Harbour, Antigua. The British colonised the islands in the 17th century and the flag's red triangles form a 'V' shape, standing for victory over colonialism.

Dominica

The stars symbolise hope and equality between the ten parishes

Green reflects the island's lush vegetation

The red disc has socialist connotations

Flag ratio: 1:2

Effective date:
3 November 1990

Use: National and civil

Area: 751 sq. km
(290 sq. miles)

Capital: Roseau

Population: 71,000

Main languages:
English, Creole

Principal religion:
Roman Catholic

Currency:
East Caribbean dollar

Dominica gained independence from Britain in 1978 and selected a new flag following a national competition.

The emblem depicts the sisserou parrot, surrounded by ten stars, which represent the island's parishes.

The cross is Christian in origin and the yellow, black and white stripes represent the Trinity. The colours are also symbolic: yellow recalls the original Carib inhabitants, sunshine and the main crops: bananas and citrus; black stands for the fertile soil and the islanders' African heritage and white represents the clarity of the water and the purity of aspiration.

The endangered sisserou parrot, unique to Dominica, is a symbol of flight towards greater heights and fulfilment of aspirations.

St Lucia

Blue stands for the sea

Black and white reflect the black and white communities and the harmony between them

Yellow represents the golden beaches

Flag ratio: 1:2
Effective date: 22 February 1979
Use: National and civil

Area: 622 sq. km (240 sq. miles)
Capital: Castries
Population: 145,000
Main languages: English, Creole
Principal religion: Roman Catholic
Currency: East Caribbean dollar

St Lucia changed hands between England and France several times before being ceded to the British in 1814.

The island is dominated by the peaks of the Pitons, rising up above the golden beaches in the south west. These are represented on the flag, which was designed by a local artist and adopted in 1967 when the country became a self-governing British Associated State.

The design of the flag was retained when St Lucia attained full independence in 1979 but the proportions of the emblem were changed and the height of the yellow triangle was increased.

The flag depicts the Pitons, twin cone-shaped volcanic formations which rise dramatically from the sea.

St Vincent and the Grenadines

Green stands for agriculture, the lush vegetation and the enduring vitality of the population

Blue represents the sky and sea

Gold symbolises warmth, the bright spirit of the people and the golden sands

Flag ratio: 2:3

Effective date:
24 October 1985

Use: National and civil

Area: 388 sq. km
(150 sq. miles)

Capital: Kingstown

Population: 111,000

Main languages:
English, Creole

Principal religions:
Protestant,
Roman Catholic

Currency:
East Caribbean dollar

Britain and France both laid claim to St Vincent, which was finally ceded to Britain in 1783.

On gaining independence in 1979 the country adopted a blue, yellow and green vertical tricolour with the coat of arms on a breadfruit leaf in the centre.

This design was not universally popular so it was replaced by the present flag in 1985. The three green diamonds form a 'V' for St Vincent, and reflect the plural nature of the islands. The diamond shapes define St Vincent and the Grenadines as the gems of the Antilles.

The leaf on the previous flag recalled the introduction of the breadfruit tree, brought to the island in 1792 to provide food for the slaves by Captain Bligh, commander of the Bounty.

Barbados

Blue represents the sea and the sky

The points of the trident represent the three principles of democracy: government of, for and by the people

Flag ratio: 2:3

Effective date:
30 November 1966

Use: National and civil

Area: 430 sq. km
(166 sq. miles)

Capital: Bridgetown

Population: 264,000

Main language: English

Principal religion:
Protestant

Currency:
Barbados dollar

A former British colony, Barbados became an independent state in 1966. The flag adopted on independence, designed by a local art teacher, was the winning entry in a competition. The trident is taken from the pre-independence colonial badge and marks the country's former links with Britain (the trident of Britannia). The shaft has been removed signifying the country's break with its colonial past. The trident is also the emblem of Neptune, god of the sea, reflecting the sea's importance in the island's economy.

The yellow band of the flag recalls the island's golden beaches.

Grenada

Green symbolises the lush vegetation and agriculture

Yellow represents sunshine, warmth and wisdom

Flag ratio: 1:2
Effective date:
7 February 1974
Use: National and civil

Area: 344 sq. km
(133 sq. miles)
Capital: St George's
Population: 92,000
Main languages:
English, Creole
Principal religions:
Roman Catholic,
Protestant
Currency:
East Caribbean dollar

Grenada, the smallest independent nation in the western hemisphere, was held alternately by France and England before being occupied by Britain in 1784.

On gaining independence in 1974 Grenada, known as the 'Spice Island', adopted a strikingly colourful flag with a stylised nutmeg in the hoist.

The red border, indicating vitality, courage and liberation, contains six stars representing five of the country's six parishes and one dependency (the southern Grenadine Islands). The central star in the red disc stands for the sixth parish, the Borough of St George's, the island's capital.

Grenada is a major exporter of nutmeg and its importance to the island's economy is reflected in the flag.

Trinidad and Tobago

White symbolises purity, hope and the waves

Red stands for the warmth of the sun and of the population

Black represents fortitude and wealth

C AMERICA

Flag ratio: 3:5

Effective date: 31 August 1962

Use: National and civil

Area: 5,130 sq. km (1,981 sq. miles)

Capital: Port of Spain

Population: 1,306,000

Main language: English

Principal religions: Christian, Muslim, Hindu

Currency: Trinidad and Tobago dollar

Trinidad, a former British possession, united with Tobago in 1889. The islands won independence in 1962 becoming a republic in 1976.

Adopted on independence, the country's flag was chosen from designs submitted by the public.

Thanks to its petro-chemical industry the nation is one of the most prosperous in the Caribbean and the flag's diagonal black stripe symbolises the islands' wealth.

A Trinidadian celebrates Carnival in Port of Spain. The vitality of the islanders is reflected by the flag's red field.

Colombia

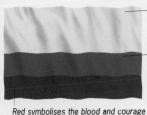

Yellow represents the golden land of South America

Blue stands for the ocean separating the country from Spain

Red symbolises the blood and courage of the people resisting the tyrants

S AMERICA

Flag ratio: 2:3

Effective date: 26 November 1861

Use: National

Area: 1,138,914 sq. km (439,737 sq. miles)

Capital: Bogota

Population: 35,100,000

Main language: Spanish

Principal religion: Roman Catholic

Currency: Colombian peso

Colombia was liberated from Spanish domination in 1819 by Venezuelan soldier Simón Bolívar and became part of the Republic of Greater Colombia along with Panama, Ecuador and Venezuela.

The yellow, blue and red tricolour – introduced by Venezuelan patriot, Francisco de Miranda – was adopted by Greater Colombia in 1819, when the yellow band was extended to cover the upper half. The design was retained by Colombia when it became a separate republic in 1830.

The flag used at sea normally bears the arms or an emblem, however this small boat is flying the plain tricolour.

Venezuela

Yellow symbolises the golden land of South America

Red stands for courage and the blood of the freedom fighters

Blue represents the ocean separating South America from Spain

S AMERICA

Flag ratio: 2:3

Effective date: 17 February 1954

Use: National and civil

Area: 912,050 sq. km (352,145 sq. miles)

Capital: Caracas

Population: 22,700,000

Main language: Spanish

Principal religion: Roman Catholic

Currency: Bolivar

Venezuela was under Spanish domination until 1821 when independence was won with the decisive victory of Simón Bolívar. Federated at first with Colombia, Panama and Ecuador as part of Greater Colombia, Venezuela became an independent republic in 1830.

The country initially used the flag of Greater Colombia, based on a design by Venezuelan freedom fighter Francisco de Miranda. In 1836 the republic reverted to Miranda's original tricolour, adding seven stars to represent the provinces which revolted against Spanish rule.

Like the flags of Colombia and Ecuador the Venezuelan tricolour is based on that of Francisco de Miranda and is closest to his original design.

Guyana

The black fimbriation expresses endurance

White stands for Guyana's rivers

S AMERICA

Flag ratio: 3:5
Effective date: 26 May 1966

Use: National and civil

Area: 214,969 sq. km (83,000 sq. miles)

Capital: Georgetown

Population: 835,000

Main languages: English, Amerindian dialects

Principal religions: Christian, Hindu

Currency: Guyana dollar

Guyana became a Dutch possession in the 17th century, but sovereignty passed to Britain in 1815. The country gained independence in 1966 and adopted this striking flag.

It was designed by Dr Whitney Smith, Director of the Flag Research Center in Massachusetts; and modified by the College of Arms, which added the black and white fimbriations.

According to Dr Smith the red triangle stands for the people's zeal in nation building; the gold arrowhead symbolises progress and the nation's mineral wealth and the green field represents Guyana's farms and dense forests.

The motif on this decorative door reflects the design of the flag, known as the 'Golden Arrow'.

Surinam

Red represents progress and love

White symbolises justice and freedom

Green stands for hope and fertility

Flag ratio: 2:3

Effective date: 25 November 1975

Use: National and civil

Area: 163,265 sq. km (63,037 sq. miles)

Capital: Paramaribo

Population: 423,000

Main languages: Dutch, Sranang Tongo, English

Principal religions: Christian, Hindu, Muslim

Currency: Surinam guilder

In 1667 the Dutch acquired Surinam (formerly Dutch Guiana) from Britain in exchange for New Netherlands (now New York). The country's name was changed to Surinam in 1948 and independence was granted in 1975.

A new flag was chosen from ideas submitted by the public. The colours represent the principal political groups, but also have symbolic significance. The yellow star stands for unity and a golden future. Its five points recall the nation's ethnic groups: Asian Indians, Creoles, white Europeans, American Indians and Chinese.

The flag is used as a wing, fin and fuselage marking by Surinam's air force.

Ecuador

A condor, poised to attack enemies, protects the nation under its wings

S AMERICA

Red stands for courage

Yellow recalls the Federation of Greater Colombia

Blue symbolises independence from Spain

Flag ratio: 1:2
Effective date: 7 November 1900
Use: National

Area: 283,561 sq. km (109,484 sq. miles)
Capital: Quito
Population: 11,500,000
Main languages: Spanish, Quechua, Jivaroan
Principal religion: Roman Catholic
Currency: Sucre

After nearly two centuries of Spanish rule, Ecuador became part of Greater Colombia, adopting the federation's flag on independence in 1830. This was virtually identical to the flag of Colombia so the arms were added in 1900.

They depict an allegorical scene: Mount Chimborazo rises above the Guayas river. In the foreground is a steamboat, its winged mast encircled by two snakes symbolising accord and trade. The blue band shows the signs of the Zodiac: Aries, Taurus, Gemini, and Cancer corresponding to the historically significant months of March, April, May and June.

The inauguration in 1996 of Abdala Bucaram and Rosalia Arteaga, President and Vice-President of Ecuador.

Peru

Red and white were the colours of the Inca Empire

Red represents the blood shed in the fight for independence

White stands for peace and justice

Flag ratio: 2:3

Effective date:
25 February 1825

Use: National and civil

Area:
1,285,216 sq. km
(496,225 sq. miles)

Capital: Lima

Population:
23,600,000

Main languages:
Spanish, Quechua,
Aymará

Principal religion:
Roman Catholic

Currency: New Sol

Spain created the vice-royalty of Peru in the 16th century. In 1820 Argentinian patriot, General José de San Martín, attempted to liberate the country, proclaiming independence in 1821. Spanish forces were finally routed three years later with the help of Venezuelan revolutionary leader, Símon Bolívar.

The Peruvian flag originated in 1820 when, it is said, José de San Martín saw a flock of flamingoes flying overhead. Assuming this to be a good omen, he exclaimed, 'Look, the flag of liberty'. His original triband, with flesh-coloured stripes, depicted the sun setting over snow-capped mountains above a still sea. The flag underwent many changes until, in 1825, the present design was specified by Símon Bolívar.

This monument commemorates General José de San Martín, one of the principal liberators of South America.

Brazil

Yellow and the diamond shape represent Brazil's mineral wealth

The motto Ordem e Progresso means 'Order and Progress'

Green stands for the vast forests

S AMERICA

Flag ratio: 7:10

Effective date:
15 November 1889

Use: National and civil

Area:
8,547,403 sq. km
(3,300,171 sq. miles)

Capital: Brasilia

Population:
155,800,000

Main languages:
Portuguese, Spanish,
French, English

Principal religions:
Roman Catholic,
traditional religions

Currency: Real

Brazil was under the rule of Portuguese king Joao VI until 1822, when he returned to Portugal leaving behind his son, Pedro I, as prince regent. Pedro declared independence in 1822 and was crowned emperor. He adopted a flag similar to the modern version, but with the royal arms in the centre of the lozenge.

Green and yellow represented the royal houses of Bragança, the ruling dynasty of Portugal, and Habsburg, house of the Empress Leopoldina.

In 1889 the arms were replaced by a celestial sphere showing the sky over Rio de Janeiro on the night of 15 November, the date when Brazil became a republic.

Independence Day celebrations in Brasilia. The stars on the sphere represent the country's 27 states.

Brazil – State flags

States are listed according to the dates of their accession.

 Alagoas
1889

Blue and red are the traditional colours of Alagoas. The arms in the centre of the flag are set within a wreath of cotton and sugar cane.

 Amazonas
1889

The large star in the blue canton represents the state capital, Manaus, while the 25 smaller stars stand for the municipalities.

 Bahia
1889

The colours are derived from a revolutionary flag of 1798 and the design recalls the Stars and Stripes. The triangle was a rebel symbol.

 Ceará
1889

Ceará used an adaptation of the national flag until 1922 when a design bearing the state arms was introduced. It was modified in 1967.

 Espírito Santo
1889

The motto, Trabalha e Confia, 'work and trust', appears in the centre of the flag. The blue and pink bands recall the evening sky.

 Goiás
1889

The stars represent the Southern Cross constellation. Green stands for the forests and gold for the mineral wealth hidden in the soils of Goiás .

 Maranhão
1889

The star symbolises the state of Maranhão as it is represented on the national flag and the stripes stand for racial fusion between ethnic groups.

 Mato Grosso
1889

The blue field represents the sky, while the white diamond symbolises peace. Green stands for the rich vegetation and yellow for gold.

Brazil – State flags

Minas Gerais
1889

The slogan of the Miners Revolt movement of 1789 surrounds the red triangle, which represents equality.

Pará
1889

Red stands for the vigour in the blood of the people. White is for the planetary belt representing the Zodiac.

Paraíba
1889

Black recalls the assassination of state president Pessoa in 1930 which led to the revolution, represented by red.

Paraná
1889

A celestial sphere appears in the centre of the flag, bearing the Southern cross and the state's name.

Pernambuco
1889

This flag, first used during the Pernambucan Revolution of 1817, was adopted by the state in 1917.

Piauí
1889

Created in 1922, the flag bears a star representing the state. The colours are derived from the national flag.

Rio Grande
do Norte 1889

The emblem of the state appears on a yellow field in the centre of the flag, which dates from 1957.

Rio Grande do
Sul 1889

The diagonally-striped flag was first adopted during the revolution of 1836. The arms were added in 1891.

Santa Catarina
1889

The lozenge shape recalls the design of the national flag. The arms were added to the centre in 1953.

São Paulo
1889

The flag symbolises the three Brazilian races: white, black and red. The canton bears a map of Brazil.

Brazil – State flags

 Sergipe
1889

This flag was originally created for use at sea and the stars represented five sand bars off the Sergipe coast.

 Distrito Federal
1960

The white field symbolises peace. The four arrows are said to represent 'the centrifugal action of power'.

 Acre
1962

The star represents the light which guided those who incorporated the state into the Brazilian territory.

 Rio de Janeiro
1975

The flag bears the arms which include elements relating to the geography, history and economy of the state.

 Mato Grosso do Sul 1977

The golden star represents the people who shine in the blue sky of hope. Green stands for the forests.

 Rondônia
1981

Using the national colours, this striking flag was the winning entry in a design competition.

 Amapá
1989

The emblem in the hoist is a plan view of the fortress of Macapá, capital of Amapá.

 Roraima
1989

The star symbolises the state of Roraima, positioned above the equator represented by the red stripe.

 Tocantins
1989

The flag is based on an ancient design. Blue and white are taken from the national flag.

Chile

White stands for the snowy peaks of the Andes

Red symbolises the blood shed by the freedom fighters

Blue represents the clear Andean skies

S AMERICA

Flag ratio: 2:3
Effective date: circa 18 October 1817
Use: National and civil

Area: 756,626 sq. km (292,135 sq. miles)
Capital: Santiago
Population: 14,200,000
Main language: Spanish
Principal religion: Roman Catholic
Currency: Chilean peso

Chile was previously under Spanish rule as a dependency of the vice-royalty of Peru. Liberation came in 1818 when the Spanish were defeated by rebel forces led by José de San Martín.

The first flag used in the struggle for independence, known as the 'Old Country', was blue on white on yellow. This was replaced by a blue, white and red flag, called 'Transition', which was used by the revolutionary troops in 1816.

In 1817 the independence movement adopted a flag similar to the present design. Reminiscent of the Stars and Stripes, it is said to have been created by US national, Charles Wood, who was serving with the rebel forces.

The star, reflected here in a glass of Chilean Chardonnay, was added to the flag on Independence Day in 1818.

Bolivia

Red stands for Bolivia's animals and the valour of the liberating army

Green symbolises fertility

Yellow represents Bolivia's mineral deposits

The scene depicted in the arms symbolises agricultural and mineral wealth

Flag ratio: 2:3

Effective date: circa 1966

Use: National and state

Area: 1,098,581 sq. km (424,165 sq. miles)

Capital: La Paz

Population: 7,500,000

Main languages: Spanish, Quechua, Aymará

Principal religion: Roman Catholic

Currency: Boliviano

Upper Peru, as Bolivia was previously called, came under Spanish rule in the 1530s and was liberated in 1825.

The flag introduced on independence was a red-green-red triband with five wreaths, each encircling a gold star – one for each of the original five departments. In 1826 the upper red stripe was changed to yellow and in 1851 the red-yellow-green tricolour was adopted.

The arms in the centre depict the mountain of Potosí – a rich source of minerals, a house, a corn sheaf, a breadfruit tree and a llama.

Bolivia was named after Venezuelan revolutionary leader, Simón Bolívar, who was known as 'The Liberator'.

Paraguay

Flag ratio: 3:5

Effective date:
circa 1990
exact date unknown

Use: National and civil

Area: 406,752 sq. km
(157,048 sq. miles)

Capital: Asunción

Population: 4,800,000

Main languages:
Spanish, Guaraní

Principal religion:
Roman Catholic

Currency: Guaraní

The colours were inspired
by the French tricolore

The Star of May
recalls the
declaration of
independence on
14 May 1811

A Spanish possession
from 1535, Paraguay
gained independence in 1811 and adopted
the red, white and blue tricolour the
following year.

The flag is unique in having different emblems on the
obverse and the reverse – a feature dating back to the regime
of dictator, José de Francia (1814-40), when the flag bore the
arms of Spain on one side and Asunción on the other.

The State Arms were added in 1821 and the Treasury Seal –
which depicts a lion sitting
beneath the motto *paz y
justicia* (peace and justice) –
was incorporated on the reverse
in 1842. Both emblems were
recently simplified.

*The plain tricolour appears on this
monument, which marks the point where
Paraguay meets Brazil and Argentina.*

55

Uruguay

The flag is modelled on the Stars and Stripes

The stripes represent the nine provinces at the time of liberation

Blue and white are the colours of Argentina and also of national hero, Jose Gervasio Artigas

S AMERICA

Flag ratio: 2:3
Effective date:
12 July 1830

Use: National and civil

Area: 177,414 sq. km
(68,500 sq. miles)

Capital: Montevideo

Population: 3,186,000

Main language: Spanish

Principal religion:
Roman Catholic

Currency:
New Uruguayan Peso

After almost two centuries of colonial rule, Uruguayan revolutionaries led by General José Gervasio Artigas ousted the Spanish in 1814. Taking advantage of Uruguay's weakened position, the Portuguese invaded in 1816, annexing the country to Brazil five years later. Aided by Argentina, Uruguay fought a successful war against the Brazilians, who recognised the nation's independence in 1828.

The flag of Uruguay recalls that of Argentina, the country's ally. The revolutionary symbol, the Sun of May, has been a national emblem since 1815.

The present form of the flag, as seen on this Uruguayan stamp, dates from 1830, although the sun emblem has occasionally been modified.

56

Argentina

The 'Sun of May' was added in 1818

The blue bands are a shade known as 'celeste', said to be the colour of the sky which inspired General Belgrano before battle

Flag ratio: 1:2
Effective date:
16 August 1985

Use: National and civil

Area:
2,780,400 sq. km
(1,073,518 sq. miles)

Capital: Buenos Aires

Population:
34,587,000

Main language: Spanish

Principal religion:
Roman Catholic

Currency: Peso

The Spanish colonisation of Argentina began in 1535 and in 1620 the region was attached to the vice-royalty of Peru.

The colours of the national flag were based on the blue and white cockades of demonstrators against Spanish rule, and represent the white clouds parting to reveal a blue sky. General Manuel Belgrano, leader of the independence movement, arranged the colours as a triband flag, which was first used at the Battle of Rosario in 1812.

The national arms are superimposed on the triband to form part of this monument marking Argentina's border with Brazil and Paraguay.

The emblem recalls the sun shining through the clouds on 25 May 1810, when the first demonstrations were held to demand self-rule.

Morocco

The 'Solomon's Seal' pentagram was added to distinguish the flag from other plain red Arab banners

AFRICA

Flag ratio: 2:3

Effective date: 17 November 1915

Use: National and civil

Area: 446,550 sq. km (172,414 sq. miles)

Capital: Rabat

Population: 27,100,000

Main languages: Arabic, Berber, French

Principal religion: Sunni Muslim

Currency: Dirham

The red flag of Morocco was first adopted by the Alaouites – ancestors of the present king, Hassan II – in the 17th century and is said to signify that the royal family are directly descended from Muhammad.

During the 19th century part of Morocco

came under Spanish rule, while France took control of the remaining territory in the early 1900s. The green five-pointed star, known as Solomon's Seal, was added in 1912 when the country became a French protectorate. The flag was only used locally until the country attained independence in 1956 and re-established a traditional monarchy.

Red is one of the traditional colours of Islam, introduced to Morocco by the Arabs in the 7th century.

Algeria

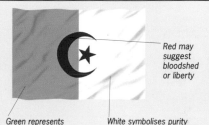

Red may suggest bloodshed or liberty

Green represents Islam

White symbolises purity

Flag ratio: 2:3

Effective date: 3 July 1962

Use: National and civil

Area: 2,381,741 sq. km (919,595 sq. miles)

Capital: Algiers

Population: 28,600,000

Main languages: Arabic, Berber

Principal religion: Muslim

Currency: Algerian dinar

O nce part of the Ottoman Empire, in 1834 Algeria was annexed by France. Although green and white were colours associated with 19th century patriot, Abd-el-Kader, it is more likely that the Algerian flag is based on a design created in 1928 by nationalist Ahmed Messali Hajd. This was adopted by the liberation movement (*Front de Libération Nationale*) in 1954 and became the national flag when Algeria gained independence in 1962.

The horns of the Islamic crescent are elongated which implies good luck and happiness.

This stamp commemorates the 35th anniversary of independence, gained in 1962 following a long and bitter struggle.

59

Tunisia

Red is an Islamic colour

The flag was introduced by Hassan II, the Bey of Tunisia

AFRICA

Flag ratio: 2:3
Effective date: circa 1835
Use: National and civil

Area: 163,610 sq. km (63,170 sq. miles)
Capital: Tunis
Population: 8,900,000
Main languages: Arabic, French, English
Principal religion: Muslim
Currency: Tunisian dinar

A former Barbary state dominated by Turkey, Tunisia became a French protectorate in 1881, although it retained its traditional ruler, the *Bey*.

The country was still nominally under Turkish rule when the *Bey* introduced the Tunisian flag in the mid-1830s. To give the nation its own identity without offending its rulers, the design was based on the Turkish flag.

Initially intended only for local use, the flag survived the period of French administration (when it was used at sea with the *tricolore* in the canton) to become the national flag on independence in 1956.

A Berber wears the Islamic star and crescent. The Tunisian flag echoes that of Turkey which is red with a white emblem.

Libya

Flag ratio: 1:2

Effective date: circa 20 November 1977

Use: National and civil

Area: 1,759,540 sq. km (679,362 sq. miles)

Capital: Tripoli

Population: 5,407,000

Main language: Arabic

Principal religion: Muslim

Currency: Libyan dinar

Green expresses the people's Muslim faith

The flag was said to represent the nation's hope for a green revolution in agriculture

In 1951 the provinces of Cyrenaica, Fezzan and Tripolitania united under King Idris I to form the kingdom of Libya.

Following a revolution in 1969 King Idris was deposed to be replaced by radical Arab nationalist, Colonel Ghadaffi, who adopted the red, white and black tricolour of the Arab Liberation movement. The hawk of Quraish was added in 1971, when Libya joined Syria and Egypt in the Confederation of Arab Republics. On leaving the Federation in 1977, Libya introduced a plain green flag, which was intended to be provisional while a new design was finalised.

Like the flag, the green uniforms and pennants of Ghadaffi's troops reflect the nation's Muslim faith. Green is also the national colour.

Egypt

Red, white and black are the colours of Arab nationalism

AFRICA

Flag ratio: 2:3

Effective date: 4 October 1984

Use: National and civil

Area: 1,001,450 sq. km (386,660 sq. miles)

Capital: Cairo

Population: 59,325,000

Main languages: Arabic, Berber, English, French

Principal religion: Sunni Muslim

Currency: Egyptian pound

Egypt was occupied by France and Britain before becoming a British protectorate in 1914. The flag hoisted in 1923, after the country was granted nominal independence, was green with three white stars within the horns of a crescent.

In 1952 the red, white and black tricolour of the Liberation Rally became the unofficial flag, with the Eagle of Saladin in the centre.

When Egypt joined Syria and Libya to form the Federation of Arab Republics in 1972 the three countries adopted a common red, white and black flag bearing the gold hawk of Quraish. Following the collapse of the Federation in 1984 the Eagle of Saladin was restored.

Saladin was a 12th century Muslim hero and his emblem, an eagle, appears in the Egyptian arms.

Sudan

White stands for Islam, peace, optimism, light and love

Black stands for Sudan and the Mahdiya revolution of the 1880s

Red recalls the martyrs of Sudan and the people's struggle

Flag ratio: 1:2

Effective date: 20 May 1970

Use: National and civil

Area: 2,505,813 sq. km (967,500 sq. miles)

Capital: Khartoum

Population: 28,098,000

Main languages: Arabic, English, indigenous languages

Principal religion: Sunni Muslim

Currency: Sudanese dinar

Formerly ruled by Britain and Egypt, Sudan became an independent republic on 1 January 1956 and adopted a blue, yellow and red tricolour.

In 1969, following a coup led by General Nimeiry, the country became a Democratic Republic and a competition was held to find a flag marking the nation's ties with the rest of the Arab world. The chosen design uses the pan-Arab colours and is based on the post-1918 Arab Revolt flag used by Iraq, Syria and Jordan.

The sails of these boats on the River Nile reflect the flag's green triangle which symbolises Islam, prosperity and spiritual wealth.

Eritrea

AFRICA

Flag ratio: 1:2
Effective date: late 1995
Use: National and civil

Area: 117,600 sq. km (45,406 sq. miles)
Capital: Asmara
Population: 3,531,000
Main languages: Tigrinya, Tigre, English, Arabic
Principal religions: Muslim, Ethiopian Orthodox
Currency: Nakfa

Green, red and blue were the colours of the EPLF flag which bore a yellow star at the hoist

A former Italian colony, Eritrea was under British and UN supervision until federated to Ethiopia in 1952, becoming a province of that country ten years later.

Prior to being annexed to Ethiopia, Eritrea had flown a flag of UN blue with a wreath and sprig of olive leaves in the centre, which survived as 'the flag of liberation' during the 31 year struggle for independence.

This emblem has been combined with the flag of the Eritrean People's Liberation Front, to form the new national flag, adopted on independence in 1993.

The olive wreath emblem, taken from the previous flag, is depicted in yellow instead of the original green.

Djibouti

White stands for peace

The red star represents unity

Green symbolises the earth

Blue recalls the sea and the sky

Flag ratio: 21:38
Effective date: 27 June 1977
Use: National and civil

Area: 23,200 sq. km (8,958 sq. miles)
Capital: Djibouti
Population: 577,000
Main languages: French, Arabic, Afar, Somali
Principal religion: Muslim
Currency: Djibouti franc

Formerly controlled by France as French Somaliland, the country became independent as Djibouti in 1977.

The two principal ethnic groups are the Issas – who form the majority and are closely related to the people of Somalia – and the Afars. The two peoples are given equal status on the country's flag, blue being the traditional colour of the Issas and green representing the Afars.

The star and triangle are adapted from the flag of the liberation movement.

The Afars of northern Djibouti are politically close to Ethiopia and have often fought fiercely with the Issas.

Ethiopia

Blue stands for peace

Red represents power and faith

Yellow stands for the church, peace, natural wealth and love

Green symbolises the land and hope

Flag ratio: 1:2
Effective date: 6 February 1996
Use: National and civil

Area: 1,104,300 sq. km (426,373 sq. miles)

Capital: Addis Ababa

Population: 56,600,000

Main languages: Amharic, Tigrinya, Galla

Principal religions: Muslim, Christian

Currency: Ethiopian birr

The Ethiopian tricolour originally flew as three separate pennants. The first single flag bearing these colours dates from 1897, when red appeared at the top and green at the bottom. The colours are those of Emperor Menelik who united the country, ruling from 1889 to 1913.

Haile Selassie succeeded to the throne in 1930 but went into exile in 1936 when Ethiopia was invaded by Italy. The present arrangement of stripes dates from his return in 1941. The pan-African colours are derived from the flag of Ethiopia, as is the flag of the Rastafarian movement, which takes its name from Ras Tarfari, as Haile Selassie was also known.

An Ethiopian human rights demonstrator. The flag's pentagram emblem symbolises the equality and unity of the people and their beliefs, while the rays stand for prosperity.

Somalia

Blue is said to represent the bright sky

The star stands for freedom

Flag ratio: 2:3

Effective date: 12 October 1954

Use: National and civil

Area: 637,657 sq. km (246,201 sq. miles)

Capital: Mogadishu

Population: 9,200,000

Main languages: Somali, Arabic, English

Principal religion: Sunni Muslim

Currency: Somali shilling

In the late 19th century north-western Somalia came under British rule as British Somaliland, while the south was controlled by Italy. Following World War II Italian Somaliland became a UN Trust Territory, adopting the current flag in 1954.

The points of the star recall the five areas inhabited by Somalis: north and south Somalia, (formerly British and Italian Somaliland), Djibouti (formerly French Somaliland), southern Ethiopia and northern Kenya.

On independence in 1960 British Somaliland was reunited with the former Italian colony and adopted the flag of the south.

Demonstrators wear the Somali colours which are based on those of the United Nations.

Uganda

Yellow stands for sunshine

AFRICA

Red symbolises the brotherhood of man

Black represents the African people

Flag ratio: 2:3

Effective date: 9 October 1962

Use: National and civil

Area: 241,038 sq. km (93,065 sq. miles)

Capital: Kampala

Population: 21,297,000

Main languages: English, Bantu, Swahili

Principal religions: Christian, Muslim

Currency: Uganda shilling

The kingdom of Buganda, in the south of present day Uganda, became a British Protectorate in 1894. By 1896 the British had extended their authority over most of the region and named the country Uganda. In 1962 the Uganda People's Congress won the elections and independence was granted later that year. The flag was adapted from the tricolour of the UPC, which had unexpectedly defeated the Democratic Party, in whose colours a new flag had already been prepared.

The central emblem shows a great crested crane within a white disc, which is taken from the colonial badge of Uganda.

Kenya

Black stands for the African people

White symbolises peace

Black, red and green, the 'black liberation' colours, denote Africa's rebirth

Red represents the blood common to all people

Green recalls the fertile land

Flag ratio: 2:3

Effective date: 12 December 1963

Use: National and civil

Area: 580,367 sq. km (224,081 sq. miles)

Capital: Nairobi

Population: 30,500,000

Main languages: Swahili, Kikuyu, Luo, English

Principal religions: Roman Catholic, Protestant, Muslim

Currency: Kenya shilling

Kenya was annexed by Britain in 1896 and gained independence in 1963, following a campaign of violence by the Mau Mau – a secret society formed by the Kikuyu tribe. In 1952 the British imprisoned Jomo Kenyatta, Kikuyu leader of the Kenya African National Union (KANU) which led the fight for liberation. He was released in 1961 and became president of the new Republic of Kenya.

The flag adopted on independence, is based on the KANU tricolour. The white fimbriations were added to acknowledge the Kenya African Democratic Union, the rival political party.

The Masai shield and spears depicted on the flag represent the defence of freedom.

Rwanda

'R' stands for Rwanda, republic, revolution and referendum

Green expresses hope for the future

Red stands for the blood shed in the revolution

Yellow represents victory over tyranny

Flag ratio: 2:3

Effective date: circa September 1961

Use: National and civil

Area: 26,338 sq. km (10,169 sq. miles)

Capital: Kigali

Population: 7,952,000

Main languages: French, Kinyarwanda, English

Principal religions: Roman Catholic, Protestant, Muslim

Currency: Rwandan franc

Rwanda was occupied by the Belgians during World War I as part of the Territory of Ruanda-Urundi and became a UN trust territory after World War II.

In 1961 the monarchy was declared a republic and gained independence the following year.

The flag adopted by the republic was a plain vertical tricolour in the pan-African colours: green, yellow and red. However the flag of Mali was modified, making it identical to that of Rwanda. Rwanda reversed the stripes and added the letter 'R' to distinguish the tricolour from that of Guinea.

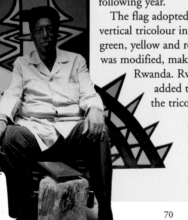

Kigeli V, former king of Rwanda. In 1961, following a series of rebellions, the Hutu, who represent 90 per cent of the population, overthrew the Tutsi rulers.

70

Burundi

Green expresses hope

White symbolises peace

It is said that the saltire may have been based on the former flag of Belgian airline, Sabena.

Red represents the blood shed in the struggle for independence

AFRICA

Flag ratio: 3:5

Effective date: 27 September 1982

Use: National and civil

Area: 27,834 sq. km (10,747 sq. miles)

Capital: Bujumbura

Population: 5,982,000

Main languages: French, Kirundi, Kiswahili

Principal religions: Roman Catholic, Muslim

Currency: Burundi franc

Urundi was administered by Belgium, together with Rwanda, as the Territory of Ruanda-Urundi. The nation gained independence in 1962, and adopted the red, green and white saltire.

The central disc originally bore a drum, and a sorghum plant. These were replaced by three stars when Burundi became a republic in 1967.

The stars stand for the words of the national motto: 'Unity, Work, Progress' and are also said to represent Burundi's ethnic groups: the Hutu, Tutsi and Twa.

Drummers in the town of Gitaga. The flag of 1962-67 bore a drum as a symbol of the monarchy which was overthrown in 1966.

Central African Republic

Red, white and blue recall the French tricolore

Red, yellow and green are the pan-African colours

Red represents the common blood of mankind which links African and European nations

AFRICA

Flag ratio: 3:5
Effective date:
1 December 1958
Use: National and civil

Area: 622,984 sq. km
(240,535 sq. miles)
Capital: Bangui
Population: 3,315,000
Main languages:
French, Sango,
indigenous languages
Principal religions:
Protestant, Roman
Catholic, Muslim
Currency: Franc CFA

Formerly a colony of French Equatorial Africa, the Central African Republic became autonomous in 1958, gaining full independence in 1960.

The flag adopted in 1958 is intended to symbolise the importance of friendship between African and European nations.

The star expresses the hope that the former states of French Equatorial Africa would establish a community as a French protectorate.

In 1966 Col. Jean Bédel Bokassa seized power and, in 1976, renamed the country the Central African Empire. He was ousted in 1979 and the country reverted to its original name.

In 1976 Col. Bokassa crowned himself emperor in an elaborate ceremony.

Democratic Republic of Congo

The small stars stand for the original provinces of Congo at independence in 1960.

The single gold star was said represent the light of civilisation

Flag ratio: 2:3

Effective date: 17 May 1997

Use: National and civil

Area: 2,344,858 sq. km (905,355 sq. miles)

Capital: Kinshasa

Population: 43,901,000

Main languages: Swahili, Lingala, French

Principal religions: Roman Catholic, Animist, Muslim

Currency: Congolese franc

Under Belgian control from 1885, the Republic of Congo achieved independence in 1960. The country's first flag was blue with a single gold star in the centre. On independence six smaller stars were added in the hoist.

When General Mobutu renamed the country Zaire in 1971 he adopted a flag in the pan-African colours. This was green, bearing a red torch within a yellow disc.

Following a coup in 1997 the country became the Democratic Republic of Congo and the flag of 1960 was restored.

The flag adopted on independence in 1960 had a paler blue field.

Niger

Orange symbolises the Sahara Desert

White stands for the River Niger

The orange disc represents the sun

Green recalls the country's forests

AFRICA

Flag ratio: 6:7
Effective date:
23 November 1959
Use: National and civil

Area:
1,267,000 sq. km
(489,191 sq. miles)
Capital: Niamey
Population: 9,151,000
Main languages:
French, Hausa, Djerma
Principal religions:
Muslim
Currency: Franc CFA

Occupied by France in the late 19th century, Niger became a colony within French West Africa in 1922.

The similarity of Niger's flag to that of the Ivory Coast reflects the countries' close economic links. The two republics both adopted new flags in 1959 and gained independence within days of each other in August 1960.

The colours of the flag are symbolic, recalling Niger's geography and natural resources.

The evening sun bathes the desert in an orange glow reflecting the colour of Niger's flag.

Chad

Red represents unity, prosperity and national sacrifice

Yellow stands for the sun and the Sahara Desert

Blue symbolises hope, the clear sky and the streams of the south

AFRICA

Flag ratio: 2:3
Effective date: 6 November 1959
Use: National and civil

Area: 1,284,000 sq. km (495,755 sq. miles)
Capital: N'Djaména
Population: 6,361,000
Main languages: French, Arabic
Principal religions: Muslim, Christian
Currency: Franc CFA

Chad was incorporated into French Equatorial Africa in 1910, becoming a separate colony in 1920. Like other African countries in the French Community, Chad attained independence in 1960.

The country's tricolour, adopted in 1959, is based on the flag of France – the former colonial power and source of continuing military and financial aid.

The colours are a combination of red and yellow, two of the pan-African colours, and red and blue from the French *tricolore*.

A Tuareg tribesman of the Sahara Desert stands silhouetted against the clear blue sky.

Mauritania

The crescent and star represent Islam

Green and yellow are Islamic and pan-African colours

AFRICA

Flag ratio: 2:3

Effective date:
1 April 1959

Use: National and civil

Area:
1,025,520 sq. km
(395,956 sq. miles)

Capital: Nouakchott

Population: 2,284,000

Main languages: Arabic, Wollof, Pular, Soninke

Principal religion: Muslim

Currency: Ouguiya

Mauritania became a colony of French West Africa in 1920 and an autonomous republic within the French Community in 1958. Full independence was achieved two years later.

Mauritania's flag, adopted the year before independence, proclaims the importance of the national faith – green and yellow are Islamic colours and the crescent and star are traditional Muslim symbols.

Green and yellow are also two of the pan-African colours, reflecting the link formed by this multi-racial nation between the Arab countries of North Africa and sub-Saharan Africa to the south.

Islam was introduced by the Arabs in the 11th century and has become the state religion, followed by 99 per cent of the population.

Mali

Green, yellow and red are the pan-African colours

The flag is modelled on the French tricolore

The design was identical Rwandan tricolour, obliging that country to modify its flag.

AFRICA

Flag ratio: 2:3
Effective date:
1 March 1961
Use: National and civil

Area:
1,240,000 sq. km
(478,767 sq. miles)

Capital: Barnako

Population:
10,795,000

Main languages:
French, Bambara,
Senufo

Principal religion:
Muslim

Currency: Franc CFA

Formerly French Sudan, the area now known as Mali joined the French Community in 1958. The following year the country formed the Federation of Mali with Senegal, proclaiming independence and retaining the name Mali when the Federation collapsed in 1960.

Mali kept the Federation's flag which bore a stylised black human figure, known as a *kanaga*. This emblem was removed in 1961, since when Mali has used a plain tricolour based on the colours of the African Democratic Rally, the leading pre-independence party.

A Peul man stands outside a mosque. The kanaga *was removed from the flag because of criticism from the country's Muslims, who disapprove of creating images of the human form.*

77

Senegal

The pan-African colours express unity with other African nations

The tricolour is reminiscent of the flag of France, the former colonial power

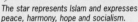

The star represents Islam and expresses peace, harmony, hope and socialism.

AFRICA

Flag ratio: 2:3
Effective date: 25 August 1960
Use: National and civil

Area: 196,722 sq. km (75,955 sq. miles)
Capital: Dakar
Population: 8,312,000
Main languages: French, Wollof, indigenous languages
Principal religion: Sunni Muslim
Currency: Franc CFA

Formerly under French rule, Senegal was granted internal autonomy in 1958. In 1959 it merged with neighbouring French Sudan (now Mali) to form the Mali Federation, under which both countries gained independence in 1960. Senegal broke up the federation shortly afterwards and became a separate republic.

The flag of the Mali Federation, initially retained by Mali, was a vertical tricolour in the pan-African colours with a black figure in the centre. Senegal kept the tricolour but replaced the emblem with a star taken from the national arms.

Examples of French colonial architecture still survive in Senegal, once part of French West Africa.

The Gambia

Red represents the sun

Blue stands for the Gambia river

Green symbolises agriculture

Flag ratio: 2:3
Effective date: 18 February 1965
Use: National and civil

Area: 11,295 sq. km (4,361 sq. miles)
Capital: Banjul
Population: 1,118,000
Main languages: English, Mandinka, Wollof
Principal religion: Muslim
Currency: Dalasi

The Gambia, one of Africa's smallest nations, occupies part of the Gambia River valley, its narrow strip of land stretching between just 24 and 48 km wide.

The country's flag, created by a local artist, deliberately avoids any political associations, reflecting the importance of the river, a significant trade artery, and the land – which is ideally suited to the cultivation of peanuts, the country's principal crop. The white fimbriations represent peace and purity.

The Gambia was formerly a British protectorate and achieved independence in 1965. This stamp recalls the year of independence as well as illustrating the symbolic meaning of the flag's colours.

Cape Verde

Blue symbolises the ocean

The stars represent the 10 main islands

The red stripe stands for the road to progress

AFRICA

Flag ratio: 10:17
Effective date: 25 September 1992
Use: National and civil

Area: 4,033 sq. km (1,557 sq. miles)
Capital: Praia
Population: 392,000
Main languages: Portuguese, Creole
Principal religion: Roman Catholic
Currency: Escudo Caboverdiano

The Cape Verde Islands were colonised by the Portuguese in the late 15th century, gaining independence in 1975.

On independence the islands adopted a flag in the pan-African colours, similar to that of Guinea-Bissau, with an emblem in the hoist featuring a black star above a yellow clam shell within a garland of maize. Both flags were based on that of the nationalist movement, the African Party for the Independence of Guinea-Bissau and the Cape Verde Islands (PAIGC).

Earlier plans for the unification of the two nations were abandoned following a coup in Guinea-Bissau in 1980 and Cape Verde broke off relations with its erstwhile partner.

The current flag was adopted in 1992.

The circle of stars represents the volcanic islands while the flag's blue field stands for the Atlantic Ocean.

Guinea-Bissau

Red, yellow and green are the pan-African colours

Flag ratio: 1:2
Effective date:
24 September 1973
Use: National and civil

Area: 36,125 sq. km
(13,948 sq. miles)
Capital: Bissau
Population: 1,098,000
Main languages:
Portuguese, Creole,
tribal languages
Principal religions:
Indigenous, Muslim
Currency: Franc CFA

The Portuguese first settled in Guinea-Bissau in 1446. Amilcar Cabral, a Cape Verdean, founded the African Party for the Independence of Guinea and Cape Verde (PAIGC), which launched a war of independence in the early 1960s.

Full independence was achieved in 1974, and Luis de Almeida Cabral, brother of PAIGC's founder, became the country's first president. The flag of Guinea-Bissau is almost identical to that of PAIGC, which is still the country's leading party.

The black five-pointed star forms the insignia of the national air-force. It represents PAIGC and the cause of African freedom

81

Guinea

Red represents work

Yellow symbolises justice

The design is based on the French tricolore

Green stands for solidarity

Flag ratio: 2:3
Effective date: 10 November 1958
Use: National and civil

Area: 245,857 sq. km (94,926 sq. miles)
Capital: Conakry
Population: 6,700,000
Main languages: French, local languages
Principal religion: Muslim
Currency: Guinea franc

Guinea was incorporated into French West Africa in the late 19th century. In 1946 ardent nationalist Sékou Touré helped found the *Parti Democratique de Guinée* (PDG) and under his leadership the country opted for full independence in 1958.

Touré was a close ally of Ghanaian anti-colonialist Kwame Nkrumah and the pan-African colours of Guinea's tricolour are derived from the flag of Ghana. The colours are also symbolic, reflecting the three virtues expressed in the national motto: *Travail, Justice, Solidarité.*

The 'wall of national heroes' in Conakry.

Sierra Leone

Green stands for the country's natural resources

White represents peace, justice and unity

Blue recalls the sea and Freetown's natural harbour

AFRICA

Flag ratio: 2:3
Effective date: 27 April 1961

Use: National and civil

Area: 71,740 sq. km (27,699 sq. miles)

Capital: Freetown

Population: 4,509,000

Main languages: English, local languages

Principal religions: Indigenous, Muslim

Currency: Leone

In 1787 the British founded a colony for freed slaves on the coast of Sierra Leone which later became Freetown, now the country's capital, and in 1896 the hinterland became a British protectorate.

On gaining independence in 1961 Sierra Leone adopted a green, white and blue tricolour, devised by the College of Arms.

This stamp celebrates the Sierra Leone-Guinea postal service, and the anniversary of the Union between Sierra Leone, Guinea and Liberia. The palm trees which form part of the emblem also appear in the national arms.

Liberia

The star depicts Liberia as a shining light

The blue canton symbolises the dark continent of Africa

The stripes represent the 11 signatories to the Declaration of Independence

Flag ratio: 10:19

Effective date:
26 July 1847

Use: National and civil

Area: 111,369 sq. km
(43,000 sq. miles)

Capital: Monrovia

Population: 2,760,000

Main languages:
English, local languages

Principal religions:
Indigenous, Muslim

Currency:
Liberian dollar

L iberia was established in 1822 by the American Colonization Society as a refuge for liberated slaves from the US.

From 1827 the colony had its own flag, clearly derived from the Stars and Stripes. This had thirteen alternating red and white stripes with a blue canton bearing a cross, which reflected the Christian faith of the Society. In 1847, when Liberia was the first black African republic to gain independence, a group of women designed a new flag which is still in use today.

Women at the Liberian National Commemoration wear dresses bearing images of American-born William Tubman, president from 1943-71 and often called the maker of modern Liberia.

Ivory Coast

Orange stands for the savannah

White symbolises the country's rivers

Green represents the forests

Flag ratio: 2:3

Effective date:
3 December 1959

Use: National and civil

Area: 322,462 sq. km
(124,503 sq. miles)

Capital:
Yamoussoukro (official),
Abidjan (de facto)

Population:
14,296,000

Main languages:
French, local languages

Principal religions:
Indigenous, Muslim

Currency: Franc CFA

A former French colony, the Ivory Coast was incorporated into French West Africa in 1904.

In 1919 the northern part of the country was detached to form part of Upper Volta, now called Burkina Faso. The Ivory Coast was declared a republic within the French Community in 1958 and gained independence in 1960.

The nation's flag is modelled on the design of the French *tricolore*.

This shield represents the Ivory Coast Olympic Committee. The national colours are shared with Niger, a fellow former member of the French Community.

Burkina Faso

Red symbolises the revolution of 1984

The five pointed star is said to signify the revolution or freedom

Green stands for the country's natural resources

Flag ratio: 2:3

Effective date: 4 August 1984

Use: National and civil

Area: 274,200 sq. km (105,869 sq. miles)

Capital: Ouagadougou

Population: 10,200,000

Main languages: French, local languages

Principal religions: Indigenous, Muslim

Currency: Franc CFA

In 1904 this former French Protectorate was incorporated into the colony of Haut-Senegal-Niger. The area was later divided between French Sudan and the Ivory Coast, and was reunited as Upper Volta in 1947.

On independence in 1960 the country adopted a black, white and red tricolour inspired by the three rivers: the Black, White and Red Volta.

In 1984, following a coup, the nation marked its break with the colonial past by changing its name to Burkina Faso. A new flag was decreed in the pan-African colours to represent unity with other ex-colonial African countries.

Once part of French West Africa, known as Haute-Volta or Upper Volta, the country was renamed Burkina Faso, meaning 'Land of the Honourable Men'.

Ghana

The star is known as the 'lode star of African freedom'

Ghana was the first country to adopt the pan-African colours

Flag ratio: 2:3

Effective date: 28 February 1966

Use: National

Area: 238,533 sq. km (92,098 sq. miles)

Capital: Accra

Population: 17,453,000

Main languages: English, French, local languages

Principal religions: Animist, Christian, Muslim

Currency: Cedi

Ghana, formerly known as the Gold Coast, came under British rule at the end of the 18th century. In 1947 Kwame Nkrumah founded a nationalist party and in 1957 Ghana became the first African nation to achieve independence in the 20th century.

The country's flag was based on the Ethiopian tricolour. In 1964 the central band was changed to white making the flag more similar to that of the ruling Convention People's Party, led by Nkrumah. However, when he was ousted in a military coup in 1966, the original design was reinstated.

A champion of African liberation, Kwame Nkrumah headed the nationalist Convention People's Party.

Togo

The white star is a symbol of hope and national purity.

Green stands for agriculture

Yellow symbolises mineral wealth

Flag ratio: 3:5
Effective date: 27 April 1960
Use: National and civil

Area: 56,785 sq. km (21,925 sq. miles)
Capital: Lomé
Population: 4,138,000
Main languages: French, Ewe, Gur, Kwa
Principal religions: Indigenous, Christian, Muslim
Currency: Franc CFA

In 1920 the former German protectorate of Togoland was divided between Britain and France. The British territory was later incorporated into Ghana while, in 1956, French Togo became an autonomous republic within the French Community.

French Togo gained independence as the republic of Togo in 1960 and hoisted a flag in the pan-African colours. The alternating green and yellow stripes represent the country's five regions while the red canton recalls the blood shed in the struggle for independence.

Independence is celebrated at this Togolese festival.

Benin

The pan-African colours express African unity

AFRICA

Flag ratio: 2:3
Effective date:
1 August 1990
Use: National and civil

Area: 112,622 sq. km
(43,484 sq. miles)
Capital: Porto Novo
Population: 5,561,000
Main languages:
French, Fon, Yoruba
Principal religions:
Indigenous, Muslim,
Christian
Currency: Franc CFA

The kingdom of Dahomey became a colony within French West Africa in 1904, proclaiming independence in 1960.

The current green, yellow and red flag was first adopted in 1959. In 1972 Mathieu Kérékou came to power and the country became a Marxist-Leninist state, changing its name to the People's Republic of Benin in 1975. Following the revolution, the republic adopted a green flag with a red star in the canton, based on that of the Marxist-Leninist party.

In 1990, when Benin abandoned its socialist policies and established a multi-party democracy, the original flag sporting the pan-African colours was restored.

This colourful stamp bears the coat of arms of Benin.

Nigeria

Flag ratio: 1:2
Effective date:
1 October 1960
Use: National

Area: 923,768 sq. km
(356,669 sq. miles)
Capital: Abuja
Population:
111,721,000
Main languages:
English, Hausa,
Yoruba, Ibo
Principal religions:
Muslim, Christian
Currency: Naira

Green stands for Nigeria's forests and agriculture

White represents the River Niger, peace and unity

The British took possession of Lagos Island in 1861 and slowly extended their control inland until, in 1914, they achieved complete domination of Nigeria. The country became independent within the Commonwealth of Nations in 1960.

The flag adopted on independence was based on the winning entry in a national competition. A red sun originally appeared on the white band, but this was omitted from the final flag.

The Nigerian flag, depicted on this stamp, was created by student, Michael Taiwo Akinkunmi. He was apparently inspired by the sight of Nigeria's forests as he flew overhead and decided to use green as a basis for his design.

Cameroon

The single star represents the unity of the former French and British territories

Flag ratio: 2:3

Effective date: 20 May 1975

Use: National and civil

Area: 475,442 sq. km (183,569 sq. miles)

Capital: Yaoundé

Population: 13,277,000

Main languages: English, French, indigenous languages

Principal religions. Indigenous, Christian, Muslim

Currency: Franc CFA

The German colony of Kamerun was divided between the British and the French following World War I. In 1960 the French zone gained independence, to be joined the following year by the southern part of the British territory (the north being integrated into Nigeria).

The flag hoisted on independence was a plain vertical tricolour in the pan-African colours. When the French and British territories formed the Cameroon Federal Republic in 1961 two gold stars were added to the red band.

In 1972 Cameroon became the United Republic of Cameroon and in 1975 the stars were replaced by a single star.

Cameroon was the second modern African state to adopt the pan-African colours, as sported by the national team in this 1994 World Cup match against Brazil.

Equatorial Guinea

White symbolises peace

Red recalls the struggle for independence

Blue stands for the sea

Green represents agriculture and natural wealth

AFRICA

Flag ratio: 2:3
Effective date: 21 August 1979
Use: National and civil

Area: 28,051 sq. km (10,831 sq. miles)
Capital: Malabo
Population: 400,000
Main languages: Spanish, Bantu, Fang
Principal religion: Roman Catholic
Currency: Franc CFA

In 1904 Bioko Island and Rio Muni became the Western African Territories, later renamed Spanish Guinea. In 1968 the country achieved independence as the Republic of Equatorial Guinea.

The country's flag bears the national arms, which consist of a silver shield bearing a green silk-cotton tree. Above the shield six gold six-pointed stars represent the mainland province and five islands which constitute the nation. Below is the national motto, *Unidad, Paz, Justicia*, 'Unity, Peace, Justice.

This stamp, issued in 1970, celebrates the nation's second anniversary of independence. In 1972, under the rule of dictator, Francisco Nguema, the flag's emblem was changed. The original design was restored following his execution in 1979.

São Tomé and Príncipe

The stars stand for the two islands

Red recalls the struggle for independence

Yellow is said to represent the country's cocoa plantations

Flag ratio: 1:2

Effective date: 12 July 1975

Use: National and civil

Area: 964 sq. km (372 sq. miles)

Capital: São Tomé

Population: 127,000

Main language: Portuguese

Principal religions: Roman Catholic, Animist

Currency: Dobra

In the late 15th century the islands of São Tomé and Príncipe were discovered by the Portuguese who brought the first settlers and set up thriving sugar plantations.

The inhabitants were subjected to harsh colonial rule and in 1960 the Gabon-based Movement for the Liberation of São Tomé and Príncipe (MLSTP) was founded to fight for independence.

When the Portuguese were overthrown in 1974, the islands provisionally adopted the flag of the MLSTP. This was retained on independence in 1975 but the central yellow stripe was widened.

This illustration, taken from a stamp issued in 1995, recalls the 20th anniversary of independence. The flag uses the pan-African colours and is based on the Ghanaian tricolour.

Gabon

Green represents
the forests

Blue symbolises
the Atlantic
Ocean

The flag's unusual 3:4 proportions are
laid down by law

AFRICA

Flag ratio: 3:4
Effective date:
9 August 1960
Use: National and civil

Area: 267,667 sq. km
(103,347 sq. miles)
Capital: Libreville
Population: 1,320,000
Main languages:
French, Bantu dialects
Principal religion:
Christian
Currency: Franc CFA

Previously part of French Equatorial Africa, Gabon became a republic within the French Community in 1958.

The flag adopted that year was similar to the present tricolour, with the French flag superimposed in the canton and a narrower central yellow band, representing the equator on which the country stands.

When independence was attained in 1960 Gabon retained the colours of the previous flag, widening the yellow stripe which now symbolises the sun.

Gabon is rich in natural resources including the dense rain forest which covers three-quarters of the land. It produces valuable hardwoods, such as that used in this example of traditional wood-carving.

94

Congo

The flag uses the pan-African colours in a striking design

Flag ratio: 2:3
Effective date: 10 June 1991
Use: National and civil
Area: 342,000 sq. km (132,047 sq. miles)
Capital: Brazzaville
Population: 2,590,000
Main languages: French, indigenous languages
Principal religions: Roman Catholic, indigenous
Currency: Franc CFA

The French colony of Middle Congo, was federated into French Equatorial Africa in 1910, gaining independence fifty years later as Congo-Brazzaville.

In 1958, the country became autonomous and adopted an unusual diagonal tricolour.

Following a Marxist revolution, at the end of 1969 the nation was declared a Communist state. A new flag was adopted in 1970, with a red field and an emblem in the canton.

A multi-party democracy was restored in 1991 and the Republic of Congo reinstated the distinctive pan-African tricolour.

Between 1970 and 1990 the flag of the communist People's Republic of the Congo bore this emblem depicting a crossed hoe and hammer within a wreath of palm fronds.

Angola

Red is said to stand for the blood spilt by the freedom fighters

Black represents Africa

The yellow of the emblem is said to denote Angola's natural wealth

Flag ratio: 2:3
Effective date: 11 November 1975
Use: National and civil

Area: 1,246,700 sq. km (481,354 sq. miles)
Capital: Luanda
Population: 11,072,000
Main languages: Portuguese, Bantu
Principal religions: Christian, Animist
Currency: Readjusted kwanza

The Portuguese arrived in Angola in 1483, but did not gain control of the country until the early 20th century. During the 1950s nationalist sentiment grew and in 1975 Angola gained independence.

The national flag is based on that of the independence movement, Movimento Popular de Libertação de Angola (MPLA), which was backed by the USSR. The emblem, which shows a five-pointed yellow star and half a cogwheel crossed by a machete, is reminiscent of the Soviet hammer and sickle.

The MPLA bicolour was based on the 18th century Anarchist flag. The red and black bands stand for 'Freedom or Death'.

Zambia

Red recalls the struggle for independence

Black stands for the Zambian people

Green represents agriculture

Orange symbolises Zambia's mineral wealth, particularly the major deposits of copper

AFRICA

Flag ratio: 2:3

Effective date: 24 October 1964

Use: National and civil

Area: 752,614 sq. km (290,586 sq. miles)

Capital: Lusaka

Population: 9,373,000

Main languages: English, over 70 African languages

Principal religions: Christian, Hindu, Muslim

Currency: Kwacha

Formerly the British colony of Northern Rhodesia, Zambia was part of the Federation of Rhodesia and Nyasaland between 1953 and 1963.

The country's struggle for independence was dominated by the United National Independence Party (UNIP) led by Kenneth Kaunda, who was elected president when Zambia became an independent republic in 1964.

The Zambian flag was designed by European artists using colours derived from the flag of the UNIP. It is unusual in having the symbols concentrated in the fly.

The eagle is taken from the national arms and signifies freedom.

Tanzania

Gold symbolises the country's mineral wealth

Blue represents the sea

Green stands for the forests and agriculture

Flag ratio: 2:3

Effective date: 30 June 1964

Use: National and civil

Area: 942,453 sq. km (363,882 sq. miles)

Capital: Dodoma

Population: 30,337,000

Main languages: Swahili, English, local languages

Principal religions: Roman Catholic, Muslim, indigenous

Currency: Tanzanian shilling

Tanganyika, once part of German East Africa, came under British control after World War I gaining independence in 1961. In 1964 the country merged with Zanzibar, to form the United Republic of Tanzania. Like the name, the flag of the new republic amalgamates elements from both countries.

Tanganyika's flag had horizontal green, black, green stripes with gold fimbriations while the flag of Zanzibar, had three horizontal stripes of blue, green and black fimbriated in white. The new flag was designed with diagonal stripes to give the two countries equal status.

The black band of the flag represents the Tanzanian people.

Malawi

Black, red and green are known as the 'black liberation' colours, recalling black activist Marcus Garvey

Taken from the arms of Nyasaland, the sun indicates the dawning of a new era

Flag ratio: 2:3

Effective date: 6 July 1964

Use: National and civil

Area: 118,484 sq. km (45,747 sq. miles)

Capital: Lilongwe

Population: 9,788,000

Main languages: Chichewa, English, Bantu languages

Principal religions: Christian, Muslim

Currency: Kwacha

Malawi was formerly a British protectorate known as Nyasaland, which became part of the Federation of Rhodesia and Nyasaland in 1953. The Federation dissolved in 1963, and the following year the independent nation of Malawi was declared.

Having previously flown the British blue ensign bearing the country's arms, Malawi adopted a new flag with no colonial connotations. The colours are those of the ruling Malawi Congress party (MCP) which led the campaign for independence.

Dr Hastings Kamuzu Banda, leader of the MCP, appears on this Malawian stamp. The country's name means 'flaming waters', recalling the sun shining on Lake Nyasa, and the rising sun appears on the flag.

Zimbabwe

Yellow stands for mineral wealth

Green represents the country's vegetation and natural resources

Red recalls the blood spilt during the liberation struggle

Flag ratio: 1:2

Effective date: 18 April 1980

Use: National and civil

Area: 390,580 sq. km (150,804 sq. miles)

Capital: Harare

Population: 11,526,000

Main languages: English, Shona, Ndebele

Principal religions: Christian, indigenous

Currency: Zimbabwe dollar

As the British colony of Rhodesia, the country flew a light blue flag with the Union Jack in the canton and a shield from the arms in the fly. In 1968, breaking with its colonial past, Rhodesia adopted a green, white, green vertical triband bearing the arms.

A black majority government was installed in 1979 and the country became independent as Zimbabwe the following year. The new flag was based on that of the leading nationalist party and uses the pan-African colours. The black-bordered white triangle represents the new leaders' desire for peace and co-operation with the white minority, while the red star denotes internationalism and socialism.

The flag has been adapted to create a logo for this taxi company. The white triangle bears the national emblem, the soapstone bird, found in the ruins of the ancient city of Zimbabwe from which the country takes its name.

RIXI TAXI

Mozambique

Green stands for agriculture

Red recalls the struggle for independence

White denotes peace

Yellow symbolises mineral wealth

AFRICA

Flag ratio: 2:3
Effective date: April 1983
Use: National and civil

Area: 801,590 sq. km (309,496 sq. miles)
Capital: Maputo
Population: 17,423,000
Main languages: Portuguese, Swahili, Bantu languages
Principal religions: Indigenous, Christian, Muslim
Currency: Metical

Mozambique emerged from four centuries of Portuguese domination in 1974, following ten years of guerrilla warfare led by the Front for the Liberation of Mozambique (FRELIMO).

During the short period of joint rule which followed, Mozambique adopted the FRELIMO flag, which was similar to that in use today.

The design was changed in 1975, but in 1983 the earlier flag was reinstated, this time bearing a Marxist star and the national emblem. This consists of a rifle which stands for defence, a book for education, a hoe for agriculture and a cogwheel for industry.

The flag's black stripe stands for the people of Mozambique. Here a woman wearing the national colours attends a rally.

101

Namibia

Blue recalls the clear sky, the Atlantic Ocean, water and rain

Red represents Namibia's people, reflecting their heroism and desire for equal opportunity

White stands for peace and unity

Green symbolises vegetation and agriculture

AFRICA

Flag ratio: 2:3

Effective date: 21 March 1990

Use: National and civil

Area: 824,292 sq. km (318,261 sq. miles)

Capital: Windhoek

Population: 1,540,000

Main languages: English, Afrikaans, German, indigenous languages

Principal religion: Christian

Currency: Namibian dollar

Formerly a German protectorate named Deutsch Südwestafrika, Namibia was seized by South Africa during World War I. An armed campaign for independence was launched in 1966 by the Marxist South-West Africa People's Organization (SWAPO). In 1968 the country was renamed Namibia and it became an independent nation in 1990, with SWAPO leader Sam Nujoma as executive president.

The SWAPO tricolour formed the basis for the new national flag, chosen from designs submitted by the public.

The new flag combines the SWAPO colours with the blue, red and white of the Democratic Turnhalle Alliance, the most important minority party. A yellow sun in the upper hoist, represents life and energy.

102

Botswana

Blue stands for water and rain

Black and white represent the racial harmony of the people

Flag ratio: 2:3

Effective date: 30 September 1966

Use: National and civil

Area: 581,730sq. km (224,607 sq. miles)

Capital: Gaborone

Population: 1,456,000

Main languages: Setswana, English

Principal religions: Indigenous, Christian

Currency: Pula

A former British protectorate, Botswana gained independence in 1966.

The country's flag is unusual in that it shows no political allegiances, but instead embodies the national motto: *pula,* meaning 'let there be rain'. Botswana has a semi-arid climate and severe droughts are a frequent occurrence. The importance of *pula,* which also stands for luck, life and prosperity, is reflected in the blue bands of the flag which represent rain and water.

The flag's black and white stripes are inspired by the markings of the zebra, the national animal.

Lesotho

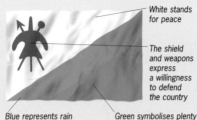

White stands for peace

The shield and weapons express a willingness to defend the country

Blue represents rain

Green symbolises plenty

Flag ratio: 9:14
Effective date: 20 January 1987
Use: National and civil

Area: 30,355 sq. km (11,720 sq. miles)
Capital: Maseru
Population: 2,050,000
Main languages: Sesotho, English
Principal religion: Christian
Currency: Loti

Lesotho was formerly a British protectorate called Basutoland, and achieved independence in 1966, when Chief Jonathan, leader of the Basotho National Party (BNP), became prime minister.

The flag adopted on independence was based on the colours of the BNP. This was rejected when Prime Minister Jonathan was ousted by a coup in 1986.

The new flag avoids political connotations by symbolising the national motto: *Khotso-pula-nala*, meaning 'Peace-rain-plenty'. The blue and green bands are not separated so that they merge when viewed from a distance. The emblem shows a traditional Basotho shield, spear and club.

The first post-independence flag bore a white emblem depicting the traditional woven straw hat of Lesotho.

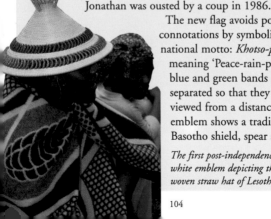

Swaziland

Blue stands for peace

The tassel is a symbol of the monarchy

Yellow represents mineral wealth

Red symbolises battle

AFRICA

Flag ratio: 2:3

Effective date:
30 October 1967

Use: National and civil

Area: 17,363 sq. km
(6,704 sq. miles)

Capital: Mbabane

Population: 908,000

Main languages:
English, siSwati

Principal religions:
Christian, indigenous

Currency: Lilangeni

Previously a British protectorate, the kingdom of Swaziland gained independence in 1968 with King Sobhuza II as head of state.

The country adopted a distinctive flag virtually identical to that given by the King to the Emasotsha Regiment of the Swazi Pioneer Corps in 1941.

The shield in the centre is decorated with a tassel made from the feathers of the widowbird and the lourie. Two more tassels hang from the fighting staff behind the shield and above the staff are two traditional Swazi spears.

The Swazi delegation at the opening ceremony of the 1996 Olympics in Atlanta. Their shirts bear the ox-hide shield, which has a pattern unique to the Emasotsha Regiment.

South Africa

Black, green and yellow are the ANC colours

Red, white and blue are the colours of the former Dutch republics

Flag ratio: 2:3

Effective date: 27 April 1994

Use: National and civil

Area: 1,221,037 sq. km (471,445 sq. miles)

Capital: Pretoria

Population: 37,900,000

Main languages: Afrikaans, English

Principal religions: Protestant, Roman Catholic

Currency: Rand

Adopted in 1928, the first flag of South Africa was based on that of the Prince of Orange, brought to the country by Dutch settlers in the 17th century.

In 1990 the government lifted its ban on the African National Congress and black nationalist, Nelson Mandela was freed after 27 years in prison. The ANC won the elections of 1994 and Mandela became president. A new flag was adopted, combining the colours of the ANC with those of the Dutch republics to reflect the new multi-racial democracy.

A choir celebrates the inauguration of President Mandela in 1994. The flag's Y-shape symbolises convergence and a united future.

Seychelles

Red reflects the people and their determination to work for the future in unity and love

White stands for justice and harmony

Blue represents the sky and the sea

Yellow symbolises the sun which gives light and life

Green recalls the land and nature

AFRICA

Flag ratio: 1:2
Effective date: 8 January 1996
Use: National and civil

Area: 455 sq. km (176 sq. miles)
Capital: Victoria
Population: 75,000
Main languages: English, French
Principal religion: Roman Catholic
Currency: Seychelles rupee

The Seychelles were settled by the French in the 18th century, passing to Britain in 1814. The Seychelles People's United Party (SPUP) and the Democratic party united to fight for independence which was granted in 1976. A coalition government was formed and the new flag combined the colours of both parties.

In 1977 the president, leader of the Democratic Party, was ousted by a coup and a red, green and white flag, similar to that of the SPUP, was substituted. The Seychelles moved towards a multi-party system in the early 1990s and the current flag incorporates the Democratic Party colours.

The giant tortoise appears on the arms of the Seychelles.

Comoros

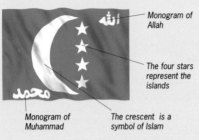

Monogram of Allah

The four stars represent the islands

The crescent is a symbol of Islam

Monogram of Muhammad

Flag ratio: 5:7

Effective date: 3 October 1996

Use: Government and civil

Area: 2,235 sq. km (863 sq. miles) including Mayotte

Capital: Moroni

Population: 653,000

Main languages: French, Arabic

Principal religion: Muslim

Currency: Comoran franc

In 1843 the French took control of the island of Mayotte, part of the Comoros archipelago, and the other three islands became French protectorates in 1886.

The country first adopted the green flag bearing a white crescent and four stars in 1963 and the islands declared independence in 1975.

In 1976 the French-speaking Christians of Mayotte elected to remain a dependency of France however the four stars were retained in the hope that the islands would be reunited.

The current flag was adopted in 1996 and includes the words Allah and Muhammad.

The position of the crescent and stars has changed several times since the flag was adopted. Between 1992 and 1996 the horns of the crescent faced upwards.

Madagascar

Red stands for sovereignty

White represents purity

Green recalls the coastal inhabitants and is a symbol of hope

AFRICA

Flag ratio: 2:3
Effective date:
14 October 1958

Use: National and civil

Area: 587,041 sq. km
(226,658 sq. miles)

Capital: Antananarivo

Population:
14,763,000

Main languages:
Malagasy, French

Principal religions:
Indigenous, Christian,
Muslim

Currency:
Franc malgache

The first inhabitants of Madagascar arrived from Indonesia and Malaysia some 2000 years ago.

The late 16th century saw the rise of a powerful monarchy within the Merina tribe, descendants of the Malay settlers who inhabited the central plateau however, in 1896, the Merina queen was exiled when Madagascar became a colony of France.

The island became a semi-autonomous member of the French Community in 1958 and adopted the flag which remains in use today.

The red and white bands of the flag, carried here at a traditional ceremony, recall the Malayo-Indonesian origins of the population.

Mauritius

Red recalls the struggle for independence

Blue stands for the Indian Ocean

Green represents agriculture and vegetation

Yellow expresses hope for a bright future

AFRICA

Flag ratio: 2:3
Effective date: 12 March 1968
Use: National

Area: 2,040 sq. km (788 sq. miles)
Capital: Port Louis
Population: 1,122,000
Main languages: English, French, Creole, Bhojpoori
Principal religions: Hindu, Christian, Muslim
Currency: Mauritius rupee

In 1721 the previously uninhabited island of Mauritius was permanently settled by the French. During the Napoleonic Wars the island passed to the British who imported labourers from India, consequently the population is predominantly of Indian descent.

Mauritius was granted independence in 1968 and adopted a flag designed by the British College of Arms. The colours are derived from the national arms.

Agriculture – particularly the cultivation of sugarcane, first introduced to the island by the French – still dominates the economy and is represented by the green band of the flag.

Iceland

Red symbolises the fire from Iceland's volcanos

White represents ice

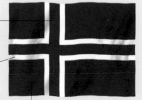

Blue stands for the mountains

Flag ratio: 18:25

Effective date:
19 June 1915

Use: National and civil

Area: 103,000 sq. km
(39,769 sq. miles)

Capital: Reykjavik

Population: 269,000

Main language:
Icelandic

Principal religion:
Evangelical Lutheran

Currency:
Icelandic króna

Iceland was under Danish control from 1380 to 1918 and first used an unofficial flag with a white Scandinavian cross on a deep blue field in 1897. This was not approved, however, because of its similarity to the Greek flag.

The current design was authorised for use on land and within Icelandic waters in 1915 by King Christian X of Denmark.

In 1918 Denmark recognised Iceland as an independent kingdom under the Danish crown and the flag was hoisted as a state ensign. Blue and white are the traditional Icelandic colours and red recalls the country's historic links with Norway and Denmark.

This stamp, issued in 1984, marks the 40th anniversary of the formation of the Republic of Iceland, when all ties with Denmark were severed.

1984

1944

ÍSLAND 50.00

Norway

Blue is taken from the Swedish arms

Red and white recall the *Dannebrog*

EUROPE

Flag ratio: 8:11

Effective date:
15 December 1899

Use: National and civil

Area: 323,877 sq. km
(125,050 sq. miles)

Capital: Oslo

Population: 4,360,000

Main language:
Norwegian

Principal religion:
Evangelical Lutheran

Currency: Krone

In 1397 Norway was united with Denmark and flew the Danish flag, the *Dannebrog*, until 1814 when the country was ceded to Sweden. The *Dannebrog* was retained with the Norwegian arms in the canton for use on land and in local waters.

The national flag was the idea of Frederik Meltzer – a Member of Parliament from Bergen – in 1821 and was based on the *Dannebrog* with a blue cross superimposed on the white. This combination of colours was popular as red, white and blue were considered symbols of liberty.

In 1844 the flag was officially recognised with the addition of the 'Union Canton', which combined the crosses of Norway and Sweden.

Norway was granted independence in 1905 and the flag of 1821 was readopted.

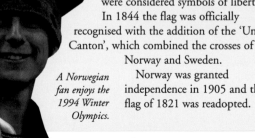

A Norwegian fan enjoys the 1994 Winter Olympics.

112

Denmark

Nordic flags bearing the Scandinavian cross are based on the Dannebrog

Flag ratio: 28:34

Effective date: 1 May 1893

Use: National and civil

Area: 43,094 sq. km (16,639 sq. miles)

Capital: Copenhagen

Population: 5,228,000

Main languages: Danish, Faroese

Principal religion: Evangelical Lutheran

Currency: Danish krone

The *Dannebrog*, or 'Danish cloth', is among the world's oldest flags.

According to legend, it appeared from heaven on 15 June 1219 during the Battle of Lyndanisse, at which King Waldemar II of Denmark defeated the Estonian heathens. In fact the design is probably derived from a flag used during the Crusades, or it may have been based on the war ensign of the Holy Roman Empire.

The flag was originally square and the cross represented Christianity. Over the years the arm at the fly was extended to form the cross used throughout Scandinavia.

The swallow-tailed ensign appears on this boathouse in Skagen.

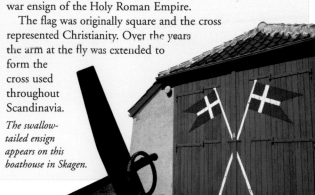

Sweden

The colours are derived from the state coat of arms of 1364

The Scandinavian cross is taken from the Danish flag

EUROPE

Flag ratio: 5:8

Effective date: 22 June 1906

Use: National and civil

Area: 449,964 sq. km (173,732 sq. miles)

Capital: Stockholm

Population: 8,831,000

Main language: Swedish

Principal religion: Evangelical Lutheran

Currency: Swedish krona

In 1397 Sweden, Denmark and Norway were united in the Kalmar Union which lasted until 1523 when, following the mass execution of Swedish leaders by King Christian II of Denmark, Gustav Vasa launched a successful revolt against the Danes.

The Swedish flag dates from this period, when it was used by Swedish nationalists in their battle for independence.

In 1523 Sweden became a hereditary monarchy under Gustav I. The anniversary of his accession is commemorated on 6 June which is *Svenska Flaggans Dag* (Swedish Flag Day).

Blue and yellow are the national colours sported in this ice hockey duel.

Finland

Blue represents Finland's 60,000 lakes

White stands for the snow which covers the ground for 5-7 months each year

EUROPE

Flag ratio: 11:18

Effective date: 1 June 1978

Use: National and civil

Area: 338,145 sq. km (130,559 sq. miles)

Capital: Helsinki

Population: 5,108,000

Main languages: Finnish, Swedish

Principal religion: Evangelical Lutheran

Currency: Markka

Finland was conquered by Sweden in the 12th century and remained under Swedish control until 1809 when it was ceded to Russia.

The country's flag was designed around 1863 by writer, Zakari Topelius. During the 19th century nationalist sentiment grew and, taking advantage of the turmoil caused by the Bolshevik revolution in 1917, the Finnish parliament took control of the country, declaring independence on 6 December 1917.

The first flag adopted sported the country's arms but this did not meet with universal approval, so the following year it was replaced by the current design.

A patriotic Finn. The Scandinavian cross recalls Finland's historical links with Sweden.

Estonia

Blue stands for faith and loyalty, the sea, lakes and the sky

White symbolises virtue, enlightenment and is the colour of snow, birch bark, and the midnight sun

Black represents past suffering and is the colour of the traditional peasant's jacket

EUROPE

Flag ratio: 7:11
Effective date: 16 November 1990
Use: National and civil

Area: 45,100 sq. km (17,400 sq. miles)
Capital: Tallinn
Population: 1,530,000
Main languages: Estonian, Latvian, Lithuanian, Russian
Principal religion: Evangelical Lutheran Russian Orthodox
Currency: Kroon

Estonia was under Swedish rule before being ceded to Russia in 1721.

The country enjoyed a brief period of independence between World Wars I and II, becoming a republic of the USSR in 1940.

The tricolour dates from 1881 when it was used by students during nationalist demonstrations. It was adopted as the national flag in 1918, going out of use when the country became a soviet republic. The flag was reintroduced in 1990 and Estonia's independence was formally recognised in 1991.

The Estonian air force, formed when the country first gained independence in 1918, uses the national colours in the form of a triangle.

Latvia

It is said that berries were used to dye the flag

Red represents the blood shed in the past and the willingness to offer it again

White stands for right, truth, the honour of free citizens and trustworthiness

EUROPE

Flag ratio: 1:2

Effective date:
27 February 1990

Use: National and civil

Area: 64,600 sq. km
(24,942 sq. miles)

Capital: Riga

Population: 2,515,000

Main languages:
Latvian, Lithuanian,
Russian

Principal religion:
Evangelical Lutheran

Currency: Lats

The earliest reference to the Latvian flag recalls a red banner with a white stripe being used by a battalion from northern Latvia around 1280. According to legend, the design was inspired by a bloodstained sheet, which had been wrapped around the wounded leader of a Latvian tribe.

The triband was adopted in 1918 when Latvia first achieved independence from Russia. In 1940 the country was annexed by the Soviet Union and the flag became illegal. It was readopted in 1990 and Latvia regained independence the following year.

Latvian flags are brandished at this rally. The triband survived as an ethnic flag while the republic was part of the USSR.

Lithuania

Yellow stands for grain and freedom from need

Green symbolises the forests and hope

Red represents bloodshed and courage

EUROPE

Flag ratio: 1:2
Effective date:
20 March 1989
Use: National and civil

Area: 65,200 sq. km
(25,175 sq. miles)
Capital: Vilnius
Population: 3,715,000
Main languages:
Lithuanian, Russian,
Polish
Principal religion:
Roman Catholic
Currency: Litas

Lithuania was allied to Poland before being absorbed by Russia in the 18th century. The country achieved independence in 1918, following the collapse of the Russian Empire, and adopted the yellow, green and red tricolour which is in use again today.

In 1940 Lithuania was annexed by the USSR. A resurgence of nationalism led to the soviet state flag being replaced by the tricolour in 1989 and Lithuania's independence was recognised in 1991.

Lithuanian ice dancers compete in the 1988 Winter Olympics. The pre-independence flag was red with white and green bands. The soviet emblem appeared in the hoist.

118

Poland

Red and white are the national colours, derived from a 13th century emblem bearing a white eagle on a red field

Flag ratio: 5:8

Effective date: 23 March 1956

Use: National

Area: 323,250 sq. km (124,808 sq. miles)

Capital: Warsaw

Population: 38,588,000

Main language: Polish

Principal religion: Roman Catholic

Currency: Złoty

Poland was once a great power, however the country disappeared in 1794 when it was divided between Prussia, Russia and Austria. Following World War I Poland gained independence and adopted the red and white flag.

The German invasion of 1939 led to the outbreak of World War II. The Germans were expelled in 1945 and the country became a police state.

In the 1980s the Solidarity trade union created the first independent political movement, winning the elections in 1989. According to Solidarity the red band of the flag stands for socialism and white symbolises peace.

The Solidarity movement, was led by Lech Walesa, who was elected president in 1990.

Germany

Black and red recall the tunics worn by soldiers during the Napoleonic wars

Gold was added to create a flag similar to the French tricolore, a symbol of revolution

Flag ratio: 3:5

Effective date: 23 May 1949

Use: National and civil

Area: 356,733 sq. km (137,735 sq. miles)

Capital: Berlin

Population: 81,642,000

Main language: German

Principal religions: Protestant, Roman Catholic

Currency: Deutsche Mark

Germany was split into small kingdoms and principalities until, in an attempt at unification, a federalist assembly met in Frankfurt in 1848, adopting the black, red and gold colours.

In 1866 Otto von Bismarck established the rival North German Confederation, which used a black, white and red tricolour. This flag was adopted when Bismarck became chancellor of the new German Empire in 1871.

After World War I the federal colours were restored, however when Hitler came to power in 1933 the black, white and red flag was reinstated – to be replaced by the swastika in 1935.

The black-red-gold tricolour was reintroduced following World War II.

The flag was retained on the re-unification of East and West Germany in 1990.

Germany – State flags

Baden-
Württemburg

The shield in the centre of the bicolour bears three lions from the arms of the House of Hohenstaufen, lords of the Duchy of Swabia.

Bayern

The pattern of blue and white lozenges is taken from the arms. The flag should bear a minium of 21, including those which are cut.

Berlin

The black bear has been the emblem of Berlin since the 14th century. The flag was that of West Berlin before the re-unification of Germany.

Brandenburg

This flag, derived from the shield, was adopted by the former East German state of Brandenburg following re-unification in 1990.

Bremen

The pattern of the flag, known locally as Gestreifter Speck (streaky bacon), dates back to 1891. The panel bears the shield of the arms.

Hamburg

The shield of the arms shows a three-towered castle. The centre tower stands for Christ and the outer two for the Father and the Holy Spirit.

Hesse

The colours of the flag are taken from the state arms. The shield appears in the centre and shows a red and white striped lion.

Mecklenburg-
Vorpommern

The flag bears a bull's head and a griffin, both local emblems, and combines the colours of Mecklenburg and Pomerania (Vorpommern).

Germany – State flags

 Niedersachsen

The flag is based on the national tricolour with the shield in the centre. This bears the white horse of Brunswick, a town in Lower Saxony.

 Nordrhein-Westfalen

The colours of the flag are derived from the arms. The shield in the centre represents the three regions which united to form the state.

 Rheinland-Pfalz

Based on the national tricolour, the flag symbolises the state's dedication to Germany. The shield in the canton represents Trier, Mainz and Pfalz.

 Saarland

Saarland was occupied by French troops following World War II, rejoining Germany in 1957 when it adopted the German colours.

 Sachsen

Saxony ceased to exist following World War II. The state was recreated on the unification of Germany and adopted this flag bearing the Saxon arms.

 Sachsen-Anhalt

The flag was originally black over yellow, however Baden-Württemburg adopted a similar bicolour so the colours were reversed in 1991.

 Schleswig-Holstein

The colours of the flag are taken from the arms of the two Duchies, as is the shield. This bears two lions (Schleswig) and a nettle-leaf (Holstein).

 Thuringia

Formerly part of East Germany, the state of Thuringia was created on re-unification and adopted this flag based on the state arms.

The Netherlands

The number of stripes changed frequently until around 1800

Red, white and blue became the colours of liberty and an inspiration for other revolutionary flags around the world

Flag ratio: 2:3

Effective date: 19 February 1937

Use: National and civil

Area: 40,844 sq. km (15,770 sq. miles)

Capital: Amsterdam

Population: 15,451,000

Main language: Dutch

Principal religions: Roman Catholic, Protestant

Currency: Guilder

In the mid 16th century the Netherlands came under the oppressive rule of Phillip II of Spain, resulting in a war of independence led by William, prince of Orange, who gave his name to the national flag. The *Prinsenvlag*, first mentioned in 1572, was an orange, white and blue tricolour.

Towards the end of the 16th century the orange stripe was often replaced by red. This was possibly because orange tended to fade in the sea air, or because new dyes produced a darker shade which appeared red. Alternatively it may have signified a shift of power to the States General, which used a red flag.

Orange remains a strong patriotic colour as reflected by the Dutch football strip.

In 1937 Queen Wilhelmina decreed that 'The colours of the flag… are red, white and blue'.

The Netherlands – Provincial flags

Drenthe

The black tower represents the fight against oppression and the stars stand for independence. Red and white were the colours of the diocese of Utrecht.

Flevoland

Blue recalls the Ijsselmeer, from which the province was reclaimed. Green and yellow represent the crops which grow on the reclaimed land.

Friesland

Using the Dutch colours the flag is said to represent the rivers and rural areas of Friesland while the lily leaves stand for the seven ancient regions.

Gelderland

The eastern province of Gelderland adopted this tricolour in 1953. The colours of the flag are derived from the provincial arms.

Groningen

The flag places green and white, the colours of the city of Groningen, within those of Ommelanden, signifying the city's central role.

Limburg

The lion is taken from the arms of the Duchy of Limburg, now divided between the Netherlands and Belgium. Blue recalls the river Maas.

Noord-Brabant

The distinctive flag of Noord-Brabant was adopted in 1959, although the design is at least 300 years old. Part of Brabant is now in Belgium.

Noord-Holland

Red and yellow are taken from the arms of Holland. North Holland's arms now also include blue, which has been incorporated to form the tricolour.

Provincial/Overseas territories flags

 Overijssel

The colours of the flag are derived from the arms. Red and yellow are the colours of Holland, while the blue band represents the river Ijssel.

 Utrecht

Adopted in 1952, the provincial flag uses the colours of the diocese of Utrecht and the archbishop's flag appears in the canton.

 Zeeland

The wavy blue and white stripes represent the sea and the crowned shield of the arms shows the lion of Holland rising from the waters.

 Zuid-Holland

The colours and arms of Holland were retained by South Holland when the County was divided and the flag is a banner of the arms.

 Bonaire

Blue stands for the sea, white for peace and yellow for the sun and nature. The red of the star within the compass represents the people's vitality.

 Curaçao

The flag's colours represent the sea, the sun and the sky. The stars stand for Curaçao and the neighbouring uninhabited island of Klein Curaçao.

 Saba

This flag was designed by an 18-year-old islander. The gold star stands for Saba while red, white and blue are the colours of the Netherlands.

 Sint Maarten

The flag uses the Dutch colours. The coat of arms appears in the hoist and below is the motto, Semper pro grediens, 'Always moving forward'.

Belgium

Modelled on the French tricolore, the vertical stripes represent liberty and revolution

The almost square proportions of the flag are unusual

Flag ratio: 13:15
Effective date: 23 January 1831
Use: National and civil

Area: 30,519 sq. km (11,783 sq. miles)
Capital: Brussels
Population: 10,113,000
Main languages: Flemish, French
Principal religion: Roman Catholic
Currency: Belgian franc

The forerunner of the current Belgian flag, created around 1790 during the struggle to expel the country's Austrian rulers, was a horizontal tricolour using colours from the arms of the provinces of Brabant, Flanders and Hainault.

Following a period of French rule from 1797 to 1815, Belgium was united with the Netherlands. The black, yellow and red tricolour was revived during the revolt against the Dutch in 1830, when Belgium declared independence. In 1831 the provisional government decreed that the colours should be arranged vertically, in honour of the French *tricolore*.

The Belgian tricolour flies alongside the flag of the EC in Brussels, headquarters of the European Union and capital of Brabant province.

Ireland

White is a symbol of peace

Green represents the Catholic people

Orange stands for the Protestants

Flag ratio: 1:2

Effective date: 29 December 1937

Use: National and civil

Area: 70,283 sq. km (27,136 sq. miles)

Capital: Dublin

Population: 3,582,000

Main languages: English, Irish

Principal religion: Roman Catholic

Currency: Punt

The Irish struggle for freedom from British rule extended over several centuries, leading to the creation of the Irish Free State in 1922.

Green, white and orange became the nationalist colours during the 19th century when they were used as rosettes and on the banners of trade guilds. Cockades in these colours were worn at a meeting celebrating the French revolution of 1830 and the French *tricolore* became the inspiration for the Irish flag.

The green, white and orange tricolour was first unveiled in 1848 by Thomas Meagher, leader of the Young Ireland movement.

The Irish tricolour expresses hope for peace between Catholics and Protestants.

United Kingdom

The red cross of St George is taken from the flag of England

The white saltire on a blue field comes from the flag of Scotland

The 'St Patrick's Cross' was, in fact, taken from the arms of the powerful Geraldine family

EUROPE

Flag ratio: 1:2

Effective date: 1 January 1801

Use: National and civil

Area: 244,101 sq. km (94,248 sq. miles)

Capital: London

Population: 58,258,000

Main language: English

Principal religion: Protestant

Currency: Pound

When King James VI of Scotland ascended to the English throne in 1603, becoming James I of England, the St George's cross and the St Andrew's saltire were combined to create a flag representing the union of the two countries. First flown at sea in 1606, the flag became known as the Union Jack, although strictly speaking when flying on land it should be called the Union Flag. The present design dates from 1801 when Ireland joined the Union and the so-called 'St Patrick's Cross' was added.

The Union Jack is not officially the national flag – although it has become so through usage – but the flag of the United Kingdoms.

UK – Sub-national flags

 England

 Scotland

The English flag is the red cross of St George, a Christian martyr who died in 303 and later became the country's patron saint. The cross first became the national emblem during the 13th century when it was worn by soldiers during the reign of Edward I (1272-1307). The St George's cross forms the basis of the flags of Northern Ireland and Guernsey. It is also the flag of the Church of England with the arms of the diocese in the canton.

The St Andrew's saltire is one of the oldest national flags, dating back at least as far as the 12th century. St. Andrew, who died around 60AD, was one of the twelve apostles who, according to tradition, was crucified on a diagonal cross. His relics were brought to Scotland and he was adopted as the country's patron saint. The cross was first used as a religious symbol, becoming a national emblem during the 13th century.

 Wales

 Northern Ireland

The flag of Wales is the Ddraig Goch (Red Dragon). The dragon is an ancient emblem, possibly dating back to Roman times. Green and white were the livery colours of the Tudor dynasty, descended from the Welsh nobleman, Owen Tudor, and at the beginning of the century the dragon was depicted on a green hill. The flag did not form part of the Union Jack since, by the Act of Union of 1536, Wales was incorporated into England.

Although Northern Ireland officially flies the Union Jack the region also has its own flag based on the arms of the province of Ulster. The six-pointed star represents the six counties and bears the red hand of Ulster. According to legend this recalls the story of a party of invaders who offered a prize to the first man to touch land with his right hand. A left-handed man cut off his right hand and threw it ashore.

UK – Sub-national flags

 Jersey

This flag is said to have arisen when an 18th century Dutch book showed a red saltire on a white field and captioned it 'Ierse' (Irish). An English writer assumed it to be the flag of Jersey and labelled it thus in his book.

 Guernsey

Guernsey originally flew the plain cross of St George. The yellow cross was added in 1985 to distinguish the flag from that of England. It is taken from the flag of William the Conqueror seen in the Bayeux tapestry.

 Alderney

A dependency of Guernsey, Alderney also flies the St George's cross. The flag bears the island's emblem. This is a green roundel with an ornate gold border and bears a lion holding a sprig of leaves.

Sark

Since the 16th century, Sark has been ruled by a hereditary seigneur or dame and the island's flag is also that of the seigneur. The two lions in the canton are taken from the arms of nearby Normandy.

 Isle of Man

The three-legged symbol, the Trinacria, dates from the 13th century but its origins are unclear. The flag is designed so that the legs run in a clockwise direction on the obverse and the reverse sides.

UK – Overseas territory flags

Anguilla (Island Flag)

Although the blue ensign became the official flag in 1980, Anguilla's original flag remains in use. The blue stripe recalls the sea and white represents peace. The dolphins stand for friendship, wisdom and strength.

Bermuda

Bermuda is unusual in flying a red, rather than a blue, ensign. The badge in the fly shows a lion holding a shield depicting the Sea Venture – a ship which was wrecked off the coast in 1609 – foundering on rocks.

British Antarctic Territory

The Territory was once part of the Falkland Islands Dependencies and the arms are based on those of the Falkland Islands. The badge depicts the snow and the sea, while the torch symbolises the search for knowledge.

British Indian Ocean Territory

White wavy lines are superimposed on this ensign's plain blue field to represent the Indian Ocean. A palm tree in the fly symbolises the islands' lush vegetation and a crown recalls the British monarchy.

British Virgin Islands

The shield shows St Ursula with eleven lamps, representing the 11,000 virgins who followed her during the Crusades. It is said that Columbus was reminded of St Ursula when he named the numerous islands.

Cayman Islands

The badge bears three stars, which represent the main islands, on a blue and white field, which recalls the sea. The motto reads, 'He Hath Founded it Upon the Seas' and above the shield is a turtle and a pineapple.

UK – Overseas territory flags

 Falkland Islands

Sheep-raising is a principal economic activity in the Falklands and a ram appears on the badge. The ship below is the Desire, *captained by English navigator, John Davies, who first sighted the islands in 1592*

 Gibraltar

The badge depicts a castle and a gold key which also appear on the flag of the City. The key represents Gibraltar's strategic position as the key to the Mediterranean. The scroll translates as 'The Sign of Mount Calpe'.

 Montserrat

The arms show a woman, Erin of Irish legend, holding a harp, and a cross, recalling the Irish Catholics who settled on the island in 1632. The cross represents the Christian faith of the inhabitants.

 Pitcairn Islands

Pitcairn Island was occupied in 1790 by mutineers of the HMS Bounty *and the anchor of the* Bounty *appears on the shield, together with the Bible. The shield's blue field represents the Pacific Ocean.*

 St Helena

The badge of St Helena shows the island's rugged coastline and a ship of the East India Company, flying the St George's cross. Ascension and Tristan da Cunha, dependencies of St Helena, also fly this ensign.

Turks and Caicos

The islands were annexed to Jamaica before becoming a British dependency. The shield bears a queen conch shell and a spiny lobster – both major exports – and a Turk's Head cactus representing the islands' plantlife.

France

Red and blue were taken from the arms of Paris

White was the colour of the Bourbon dynasty

Flag ratio: 2:3

Effective date: 5 March 1848

Use: National and civil

Area: 551,500 sq. km (212,935 sq. miles)

Capital: Paris

Population: 58,143,000

Main language: French

Principal religion: Roman Catholic

Currency: Franc

The colours of the French *tricolore* first appeared during the revolution of 1789 when King Louis XVI visited Paris, days after the storming of the Bastille. He wore a cockade combining the colours of the monarchy and the arms of Paris, signifying reconciliation between royalty and the city.

The cockade was quickly adopted by the revolutionaries and the *tricolore* was created In 1790, replacing the white standard of the Bourbons.

It was first used as a canton on naval flags when the colours were reversed. The present flag dates from 1794, going out of use in 1814 when Napoleon was defeated at Waterloo, but reintroduced in 1830.

A patriotic supporter celebrates France's victory in the 1998 World Cup.

Luxembourg

The blue band is lighter than that of the Dutch tricolour

Flag ratio: 3:5
Effective date:
16 August 1972
Use: National

Area: 2,586 sq. km
(998 sq. miles)
Capital: Luxembourg
Population: 406,000
Main languages:
French, German,
Luxembourg
Principal religions:
Roman Catholic
Currency:
Luxembourg franc

Between 1448 and 1814 Luxembourg was ruled by Burgundy, Spain, Austria, and France, becoming a grand-duchy under William I, king of the Netherlands, in 1815.

The flag of Luxembourg is almost identical to the Dutch tricolour, differing only in the proportions and the shade of blue. In spite of the two countries' historical links, the similarity is coincidental and the colours have different origins. The flag of Luxembourg is derived from the coat of arms which shows a red lion against a blue and white striped field.

The arms of the Grand-Duke of Luxembourg are displayed on this Californian car.

Monaco

The flag's colours date back to the 14th century

The bicolour is identical to that of Indonesia except in its ratio

EUROPE

Flag ratio: 4:5
Effective date: 4 April 1881
Use: National and civil

Area: 1 sq. km (0.4 sq. miles)
Capital: Monaco
Population: 31,000
Main language: French
Principal religion: Roman Catholic
Currency: French franc

The tiny principality of Monaco has belonged to the Grimaldi family of Genoa since 1297, except during the French revolution when it was annexed to France.

In 1815 the country became a Sardinian protectorate and it was not re-established as an independent state until 1861.

The colours of the flag are derived from the arms of the house of Grimaldi.

A sentry guards the Royal Palace. Prince Rainier III of the Grimaldi family has ruled the principality since 1949.

Andorra

Red and yellow represent the influence of Spain

Blue and red acknowledge Andorra's links with France

Flag ratio: 2:3

Effective date: circa 1866

Use: National

Area: 453 sq. km (175 sq. miles)

Capital: Andorra la Vella

Population: 68,000

Main languages: Catalan, French, Castillian

Principal religion: Roman Catholic

Currencies: French franc, Spanish peseta

In 1278 this small principality came under the joint rule of the Catalan bishop of Urgel and the French count of Foix.

The bishop and the French president still function jointly as heads of state and this is reflected in the colours of Andorra's flag.

The coat of arms appears in the centre of the tricolour: on the left the Bishop of Urgel is represented by the crozier and mitre, and the four red stripes below are taken from the arms of Catalonia; on the right three red stripes stand for the Count of Foix and the two cows are part of the arms of Béarne.

The colours of the Andorran flag are reflected in this postage stamp.

Portugal

Green and red replaced blue and white as the national colours in 1910

The armillary sphere surrounds the shield of Portugal

Flag ratio: 2:3

Effective date: 30 June 1911

Use: National and civil

Area: 91,932 sq. km (35,514 sq. miles)

Capital: Lisbon

Population: 10,797,000

Main language: Portuguese

Principal religion: Roman Catholic

Currency: Escudo

In the 15th century a series of overseas conquests directed by Prince Henry the Navigator made Portugal one of the greatest colonial powers in the world.

The kingdom became a republic in 1910, following a coup which ousted King Manuel II, and the current green and red flag was adopted.

Green is said to stand for Henry the Navigator and red for the revolution. However red and green may reflect the colours of the *Carbonarians* (charcoal burners), a Portuguese republican movement.

The armillary sphere symbolises Portugal's voyages of discovery.

The armillary sphere is a medieval navigational instrument.

Spain

The Pillars of Hercules, represent the promontories of Gibraltar and Ceuta

The shield represents the regions of Castile, León, Aragón, Navarre and Granada

Flag ratio: 2:3

Effective date:
18 December 1981

Use:
National and state

Area: 505,992 sq. km
(195,365 sq. miles)

Capital: Madrid

Population:
39,210,000

Main languages:
Spanish, Catalan,
Galician, Basque

Principal religion:
Roman Catholic

Currency: Peseta

In the 15th century the kingdoms of Castile in the west of Spain and Aragón in the east were united by the marriage of Isabella I and Ferdinand II. Red and yellow were the heraldic colours of Castile and Aragón and, in 1785, a red and yellow flag was adopted by Charles III for use at sea.

Spain became a republic in 1931 and the republican flag, a red, yellow and purple horizontal tricolour, was introduced. Army officers under Francisco Franco revolted against the government, overthrowing the republic in 1939, when the red and yellow flag was restored.

Red and yellow, the traditional Spanish colours, are based on those adopted by Aragón and Castile.

Spain – Regional flags

 Andalusia

The flag's colours date from the 18th century. The emblem includes the Lions of Cadiz and, like the national arms, the Pillars of Hercules.

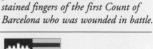 Aragón

According to legend the stripes recall a golden shield marked by the blood-stained fingers of the first Count of Barcelona who was wounded in battle.

Asturias

The Greek letters alpha and omega hung from the 'Victory Cross', a traditional symbol, representing God, the beginning and the end.

Baleares

The flag of the Balearic Islands, captured in 1235 by James I of Aragón, is based on that of Aragón and bears the emblem of Palma.

 Cantabria

The flag of the local independence movement, which bears a celtic symbol, was rejected in favour of this design, based on a maritime ensign.

 Castilla-La Mancha

The castle on a red field is the traditional emblem of Castilla, which also appears in the national arms and on the flag of Castilla y León.

 Castilla y León

The castles represent Castilla, while the two lions stand for León. The neighbouring regions were permanently united in 1230.

 Catalunya

Catalonia was united with the kingdom of Aragón in 1137 and the two regions' red and yellow striped flags share the same origins.

Spain – Regional flags

 Extremadura

The colours are traditional, standing for faith, truth and courage. The arms include a cork oak tree.

 Galicia

The arms and the colours of the flag, which recall the Virgin Mary, represent the Galicians' Catholic faith.

 Islas Canarias (Canary Islands)

The colours are said to recall the white sand, blue sea and golden sunshine which attract tourists to the islands.

 Madrid

Taken from the arms, the stars stand for Madrid's seven districts. The city of Madrid flies a different flag.

 Murcia

The four castles recall Castilla, which annexed the region in 1243. Seven crowns represent Murcia's provinces.

 Navarre

The emblem and the colour of the flag are traditional, dating back to the 14th century.

 País Vasco (Basque Country)

Red is a traditional colour. The white cross represents Christianity while the saltire stands for Basque freedom.

 La Rioja

The colours of the flag are derived from the regional arms, which appear in the centre.

 Valencia

Once ruled by El Cid, Valencia was united with Aragón in 1319, a link recalled by the red and yellow stripes.

Italy

The colours of the flag date from Napoleon's invasion in 1796

The design is based on the French tricolore

Flag ratio: 2:3
Effective date: 19 June 1946
Use: National

Area: 301,268 sq. km (116,320 sq. miles)
Capital: Rome
Population: 57,187,000
Main language: Italian
Principal religion: Roman Catholic
Currency: Lira

Italy was a collection of independent states when Napoleon invaded in 1796. His conquests led to the formation of the Cisalpine Republic which adopted a green, white and red tricolour.

In 1805 Napoleon became king of Italy and his arms were added to the flag, but following his defeat in 1815 the tricolour went out of use.

When the kingdom of Italy was proclaimed in 1861 the tricolour was readopted bearing the arms of Savoy. The country became a republic in 1946 and the arms were removed.

The Italian colours, which appear on this football club badge, were adapted from the French tricolore. It is said that green was substituted for blue because it was Napoleon's favourite colour.

Vatican City

The emblem reflects the Vatican's importance as the headquarters of the Roman Catholic church

The colours of the flag are based on the gold and silver of the papal keys

EUROPE

Flag ratio: 1:1

Effective date:
8 June 1929

Use: Civil

Area: 0.44 sq. km
(0.17 sq. miles)

Population: 1,000

Main languages:
Italian, Latin

Principal religion:
Roman Catholic

Currency: Lira

In 1870 the Papal States, which once incorporated almost all of central Italy, became part of newly-united Kingdom of Italy, however the Vatican remained under the jurisdiction of the pope.

Vatican City became an independent state in 1929, its population consisting mainly of employees of the Holy See, the government of the Roman Catholic church.

The state's flag is square and bears a 13th century emblem showing the papal crown supported by crossed gold and silver keys. These are the symbol of St Peter, traditionally the first bishop of Rome and keeper of the keys to heaven.

Welcoming the Pope – yellow and white have been the papal colours since the 19th century.

Malta

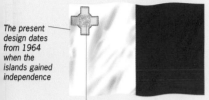

The present design dates from 1964 when the islands gained independence

The George Cross was awarded by King George VI and originally appeared in a small blue canton

Flag ratio: 2:3

Effective date: 21 September 1964

Use: National

Area: 316 sq. km (122 sq. miles)

Capital: Valletta

Population: 371,000

Main languages: Maltese, English

Principal religion: Roman Catholic

Currency: Maltese lira

The republic of Malta consists of the islands of Malta, Gozo and Comino. Their strategic location attracted a number of foreign invaders before the country was granted to the Knights of St John of Jerusalem in 1530. The islands were seized by Napoleon in 1798 and elected to become part of the British Empire in 1814.

According to legend the flag is based on the colours of the Norman count who conquered Malta in 1090. The George Cross was added in 1943 to mark the heroism of the Maltese under daily bombing by Germany and Italy during World War II.

Red and white were the colours of the shield of the Knights of St John, however the colours of the flag are said to date from the Norman conquest.

San Marino

Blue stands for the sky

White represents the snow on Mount Titano and the clouds above

Flag ratio: 3:4

Effective date:
6 April 1862

Use: National and state

Area: 61 sq. km
(24 sq. miles)

Capital: San Marino

Population: 25,000

Main language: Italian

Principal religion:
Roman Catholic

Currencies: San
Marino lira, Italian
lira

Founded in the 4th century, the tiny republic of San Marino is totally surrounded by Italy. Despite repeated incursions by neighbouring armies the country has maintained its autonomy and claims to be the oldest independent state in Europe.

The republic's blue and white flag was first mentioned in 1797 following Napoleon's invasion of Italy.

2 MARZO 1992   INGRESSO
DI SAN MARINO ALL'ONU

1000

SAN MARINO

The arms, which appear on this stamp and in the centre of the flag, show three mountain peaks, each topped by a tower bearing an ostrich feather. These represent the citadels of Montale, Cesta and Guaita, which are situated on Mount Titano.

Switzerland

The flag may have been based on that of Schwyz, one of the original cantons of the Confederation

While the national flag is square, a rectangular flag is used on Swiss lakes and rivers

Flag ratio: 1:1

Effective date: 12 December 1889

Use: National and civil

Area: 41,288 sq. km (15,941 sq. miles)

Capital: Berne

Population: 7,040,000

Main languages: German, French, Italian, Romansch

Principal religion: Roman Catholic, Protestant

Currency: Swiss franc

Formerly the Roman province of Helvetica, Switzerland was founded in 1291 when the cantons of Schwyz, Uri and Unterwalden formed a defensive alliance which was later joined by other districts.

In 1648 the Swiss Confederation achieved independence from the Holy Roman Empire. Although not officially adopted until 1848, the Confederation's flag dates from the 14th century when soldiers at the Battle of Laupen were distinguished by white crosses on red shields.

Famed for its neutrality, the country is the headquarters of the International Red Cross, and the organisation's flag is based on that of Switzerland.

The Swiss flag is displayed before a World Cup match.

Switzerland – Canton flags

 Aargau

The stars represent the three districts which united to form the canton of Aargau, while the blue and white wavy lines stand for the River Aare. The stars sometimes appear on a paler blue field.

 Appenzell Ausser-Rhoden

The canton of Appenzell was divided in the late 16th century to form two half-cantons. The initials VR, which stood for Usser-Rhoden, differentiate the flag from that of Inner-Rhoden.

 Appenzell Inner-Rhoden

The original flag of Appenzell, which joined the Swiss Confederation in the early 16th century, was retained by Appenzell Inner-Rhoden when the canton was divided in 1597. The bear emblem dates from medieval times.

 Basel-Land

The half-canton of Basel-Land (or Basel-Landschaft) was created from the former canton of Basel in 1833. The city of Basel was formerly ruled by bishops and the bishop's crozier, or staff, is an ancient emblem.

 Basel-Stadt

Previously part of the canton of Basel, which joined the Swiss Confederation in 1501, the half-canton of Basel-Stadt retained the bishop's crozier emblem in its original form when the canton was divided in 1833

 Bern

A bear has been the canton's heraldic emblem since the 12th century, and a bear pit, dating from medieval times, has been preserved in the city of Bern. Bär, the German word for bear, recalls the name of the canton.

Switzerland – Canton flags

 Fribourg

Black and white have been the canton's colours since the 15th century and the simple bicolour is derived from the coat of arms. Fribourg became a member of the Swiss Confederation in 1831.

 Genève

In the 10th and 11th centuries Switzerland was under the rule of the Holy Roman Empire, which is recalled in the flag of Geneva by the black eagle. The golden Key of St Peter appears in the fly.

 Glarus

The flag depicts the figure of St Fridolin, patron saint of the canton, holding his walking stick and Bible as he watches over his land and its people. The canton became a member of the Confederation in 1352.

 Graubünden

The flag is composed of the emblems of three medieval leagues: the Grey League, the League of God's House and the League of Ten Jurisdictions, which united to form a federated state, becoming a canton in 1854.

 Jura

Jura, which was originally part of Bern, became the newest canton of the Confederation on 1 January 1979. The flag's red and white stripes are derived from the arms and the bishop's crozier recalls Basel.

 Luzern

Blue and white are the colours of the shield of the canton's arms, and are arranged horizontally in the flag, rather than vertically as in the arms. Luzern joined the Confederation during the 14th century.

Switzerland – Canton flags

 Neuchâtel

The cross represents Switzerland, and the colours date from 1848, when the republican flag was based on that of Italian independence movement.

 Nidwalden

Nidwalden was formed when the canton of Unterwalden was divided in 1815. The canton's emblem is the Key of St Peter.

 Obwalden

Obwalden was formerly part of Unterwalden, one of the original members of the Confederation, and has retained Unterwalden's emblem.

 Sankt Gallen

On its formation in 1803, the canton adopted the axe and fasces (a bundle of wooden rods) – an ancient Roman symbol of republicanism.

 Schaffhausen

Schaf is German for sheep and a ram is the emblem of this canton, which entered the Swiss Confederation at the beginning of the 16th century.

 Schwyz

A white cross was added to the canton's original red flag during the 14th century. The national flag may have been based on that of Schwyz.

 Solothurn

The bicolour is derived from the coat of arms. The colours are those of the Swiss Confederation, joined by the canton during the 15th century.

 Thurgau

The lions – taken from arms granted to Thurgau in 1094 – appeared on a black, then a red, flag before the current version was approved in 1803.

Switzerland – Canton flags

 Ticino

Swiss troops annexed the Italian districts and towns that later formed the canton of Ticino in the 16th century. The canton's flag arranges red and blue, taken from the shield of the arms, as a horizontal bicolour.

 Uri

One of the original three cantons of the Confederation, Uri has a distinctive flag bearing the head of an auroch, an extinct long-horned wild ox, which has been the canton's emblem since the 13th century.

 Valais

Valais, known in German as Wallis, joined the Swiss Confederation at the beginning of the 19th century. The flag is based on the coat of arms, and the stars represent the communes which made up the canton.

 Vaud

The motto reads: Liberté et Patrie, 'Freedom and Fatherland', and freedom is also represented by the flag's colours. The lettering appears with and without an outline and a plain bicolour is also sometimes used.

 Zug

Zug joined the Swiss Confederation in the 14th century, and adopted the blue and white triband. Formerly under Habsburg rule, the canton's original flag was red and white, based on the Austrian colours.

Zürich

Blue and white have been the colours of the canton of Zürich since the 13th century and also appear in the same form on the shield of the coat of arms. Zürich joined the Swiss Confederation in 1351.

Liechtenstein

The crown emblem was modernised in 1982

The colours date back to the 18th century

Flag ratio: 3:5
Effective date: 18 September 1982
Use: National and civil

Area: 160 sq. km (62 sq. miles)
Capital: Vaduz
Population: 31,000
Main languages: German, Alemannish
Principal religion: Roman Catholic
Currency: Swiss franc

Once part of the Holy Roman Empire, the independent principality of Liechtenstein was established in 1719.

In 1921 the country adopted a simple blue and red bicolour. However at the 1936 Olympic Games it was noted that this was very similar to the flag of Haiti, so the yellow crown – which represents the Prince of Liechtenstein – was added to the upper hoist.

The flag is often hung from a horizontal staff and an alternative version exists with the crown turned 90 degrees anti-clockwise so that it remains upright.

The principality's flag appears on this stamp, issued in 1981. The origin of the national colours is unknown.

Austria

Red and white have been Austria's national colours for over 800 years

EUROPE

Flag ratio: 2:3
Effective date:
27 April 1984

Use: National and civil

Area: 83,849 sq. km
(32,374 sq. miles)
Capital: Vienna
Population: 8,053,000
Main language:
German
Principal religion:
Roman Catholic
Currency: Schilling

The Austrian flag is one of the oldest in the world. According to legend, the red and white bands were inspired by the blood-stained tunic of Leopold, Duke of Babenberg, who fought so ferociously at the Battle of Ptolemais in 1191 that the only part of his costume to remain white was the area covered by his belt.

Use of the flag was banned following the *Anschluß* in 1938, when Austria became a German state under the authority of the Third Reich, but it was restored when the country was liberated in 1945.

The two-headed eagle was an emblem used by the Habsburgs. A single-headed eagle now appears in the Austrian arms.

Austria – State flags

 Burgenland

Red and yellow are derived from the shield of the arms which often appears in the centre of the flag.

 Kärnten

The colours of the Carinthian flag are taken from the shield of the coat of arms, which bears three black lions.

 Nieder-Österreich

The colours of the flag of Lower Austria are those of the arms which feature golden eagles on a blue field.

Ober-Österreich

The bicolour of Upper Austria uses the national colours, which are also those of the state arms.

 Salzburg

The flag of Salzburg is based on the national colours. It sometimes bears a simple crown emblem.

Steiermark

Styria changed its colours to green and white after separating from the Duchy of Carinthia in 1180.

 Tirol

The flag often bears a red eagle in a white disc. The plain bicolour is identical to that of Upper Austria.

 Vorarlberg

This bicolour, which is identical to the flags of Salzburg and Vienna, is derived from the state arms.

 Wien

Identical to the flags of Salzburg and Vorarlberg, the bicolour of Vienna is based on the state arms.

Hungary

Red stands for strength

White symbolises faithfulness

Green represents hope

EUROPE

Flag ratio: 2:3

Effective date: 1 October 1957

Use: National and civil

Area: 93,030 sq. km (35,919 sq. miles)

Capital: Budapest

Population: 10,319,000

Main languages: Hungarian, German

Principal religion: Roman Catholic

Currency: Forint

The colours of the flag can be traced back to Arpad, 9th century leader of the Magyars and a legendary national hero.

In 1608 red, white and green were used at the coronation of King Matthias II and became the colours of the country's arms. They were suppressed under Habsburg rule, but reappeared during the revolution of 1848 in the form of a tricolour, inspired by the French flag. The royal crown was added to the central band, to be replaced by the national arms in 1945.

When Hungary came under Communist rule in 1949 a Soviet-style emblem was substituted. The plain tricolour was adopted following the revolt of 1956.

During the uprising of 1956 the soviet emblem was cut from the flag leaving a hole.

Czech Republic

Red and white are the colours of Bohemia, dating back to the 13th century

Blue represents Moravia

Unlike that of Slovakia the Czech flag is not based on the pan-Slav colours

Flag ratio: 2:3
Effective date: 1 January 1993
Use: National and civil

Area: 78,864 sq. km (30,449 sq. miles)
Capital: Prague
Population: 10,331,000
Main language: Czech
Principal religion: Roman Catholic
Currency: Koruna

The Czech Republic – which includes the provinces of Bohemia and Moravia – united with Slovakia to form Czechoslovakia in 1918. The Czechoslovak flag was based on the arms of Bohemia, which were red and white. However, since the white and red bicolour was identical to the flag of Poland, a blue triangle was added in the hoist, blue being one of the colours of Moravia and Slovakia.

When the Czech Republic separated from Slovakia in 1993 the Czechs retained the flag, despite a resolution that both states should adopt a new design.

Flag-waving crowds gather round the statue of Vaclav Wenceslas, patron saint of Bohemia.

Slovakia

The arms depict the Carpathian mountains which traverse Slovakia

The flag uses the pan-Slav colours representing liberation from foreign domination

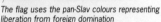

Flag ratio: 2:3

Effective date: 3 September 1992

Use: National and civil

Area: 49,012 sq. km (18,924 sq. miles)

Capital: Bratislava

Population: 5,364,000

Main languages: Slovak, Hungarian, Czech

Principal religion: Roman Catholic

Currency: Koruna

In 1919 Slovakia, formerly under Hungarian rule, united with the Czech Republic to form Czechoslovakia.

As part of Czechoslovakia Slovakia used the flag currently flown by the Czech Republic. However, during the second world war, encouraged by the Germans, Slovakia formed a republic and adopted a flag similar to the present tricolour, with the arms in the centre.

On the collapse of Czechoslovakia in 1993, Slovakia readopted the tricolour placing the arms towards the hoist.

Blood-stained pan-Slav flags are raised in protest during the 1968 Soviet invasion of Bratislava.

Slovenia

The three stars are taken from the arms of the Duchy of Selje

The flag uses the pan-Slav colours

EUROPE

Flag ratio: 1:2

Effective date:
25 June 1991

Use: National and civil

Area: 20,256 sq. km
(7821 sq. miles)

Capital: Ljubljana

Population: 1,984,000

Main languages:
Slovene, Hungarian

Principal religion:
Roman Catholic

Currency: Tolar

Slovenia was under Austrian rule before becoming part of Yugoslavia in 1918. The country's flag dates back to the mid-19th century when the Slovenes were inspired by the white, red and blue Russian tricolour – anticipating support in their fight for liberation from Austria.

The province of Slovenia retained the colours while part of Yugoslavia, adding a gold-rimmed red star in the centre of the flag.

On independence in 1991 the star was replaced by the coat of arms which depicts the mountainous landscape and the waves of the Adriatic coast.

The Slovenian declaration of independence in 1991 helped trigger the Yugoslav civil war.

Croatia

Red, white and blue are the pan-Slav colours

The small shields represent Croatia Ancient, Dubrovnik, Dalmatia, Istria and Slavonia

The flag is based on the tricolour used during World War II

Flag ratio: 1:2

Effective date:
22 December 1990

Use: National and civil

Area: 88,117 sq. km
(34,022 sq. miles)

Capital: Zagreb

Population: 4,495,000

Main language:
Croato-Serb

Principal religion:
Roman Catholic

Currency: Kuna

Formerly ruled by Hungary and Austria, Croatia unofficially adopted the pan-Slav tricolour in the mid-19th century. The region joined Yugoslavia in 1919, becoming a nominally independent state under German and Italian domination during the second world war, when the arms were added to the flag.

Following the war, as a republic of communist Yugoslavia, Croatia continued to use the tricolour with a red star fimbriated in gold in place of the arms.

In 1990 nationalist, Franjo Tudjman, was elected president and the current flag was introduced. Independence was declared in 1991.

This 18th century engraving shows an early Croatian flag.

Bosnia Herzegovina

The stars on a blue field represent Europe

The yellow triangle stands for equality between the three peoples of Bosnia Herzegovina

Flag ratio: 1:2
Effective date: 4 February 1998
Use: National and civil

Area: 51,128 sq. km (19,741 sq. miles)
Capital: Sarajevo
Population: 4,484,000
Main language: Croato-Serb
Principal religions: Muslim, Orthodox Christian, Roman Catholic
Currency: Convertible marka

Formerly part of the Ottoman Empire, in 1908 Bosnia Herzegovina came under the control of Austria-Hungary. After World War I the country was incorporated into Yugoslavia, declaring independence in 1992.

The flag adopted in 1991 bore the arms of 14th century king Stephen Tvrtko on a white field.

Nova uniforma poštara BiH

1.00

◆ BOSNA I HERCEGOVINA

In 1998 the United Nations High Representative imposed a new neutral flag in time for the Winter Olympics. In fact, four flags are currently in use since the Serbs and the Croats each have their own flags, while the country's Muslims still favour the previous design.

The latest uniforms of the postal service echo the colours of the new flag.

Yugoslavia

Blue, white and red recall the 19th century Russian tricolour

The 'Partisan Star' was removed in 1991

Flag ratio: 1:2

Effective date: 27 April 1992

Use: National and civil

Area: 102,173 sq. km (39,449 sq. miles)

Capital: Belgrade

Population: 10,544,000

Main languages: Serbo-Croat, Macedonian, Hungarian, Albanian

Principal religions: Orthodox Christian, Roman Catholic, Muslim

Currency: New dinar

Yugoslavia was formed following the collapse of the Austro-Hungarian empire in 1918, and adopted the blue, white and red tricolour, representing pan-Slav unity.

When the country became a communist republic in 1946, a gold-edged red star – a war-time communist partisan badge – was added to the flag. During 1991-92 four of the Yugoslav republics declared independence while Serbia and Montenegro, established the Federated Republic of Yugoslavia, retaining the tricolour without the star.

Chetniks sell Serbian nationalist flags and icons on the streets of Belgrade.

Albania

Red represents the blood shed during the fight for independence

According to legend Albanians are descended from the eagle, which is the national emblem

Flag ratio: 5:7
Effective date:
22 May 1993
Use: National

Area: 28,748 sq. km
(11,100 sq. miles)
Capital: Tirana
Population: 3,645,000
Main languages:
Albanian, Greek
Principal religions:
Muslim,
Greek Orthodox,
Roman Catholic
Currency: Lek

Albania, once part of the Byzantine empire, gained independence in 1912 when the country adopted the red flag bearing a two-headed eagle.

The eagle dates back to the 15th century when Albanian, Gjergj Kastrioti, was taken hostage by the Turks, becoming a general in their army under the name Skanderbeg. In 1443 he

returned to lead the Albanians in battle and expelled the Turkish invaders. He was glorified as a national hero and the eagle, which featured on his seal, was adopted as Albania's emblem.

When the country became a communist republic in 1946 a yellow star was added above the eagle, but this was removed in 1992 by order of the new regime.

Shqipëria, *the Albanian name for the country, means 'land of the eagle'.*

Macedonia

Red and yellow were the colours of Macedonia's flag when the republic was part of Yugoslavia

Flag ratio: 1:2

Effective date:
6 October 1995

Use: National and civil

Area: 25,713 sq. km
(9928 sq. miles)

Capital: Skopje

Population: 2,163,000

Main languages:
Macedonian, Albanian,
Turkish, Serbo-Croat

Principal religions:
Eastern Orthodox,
Muslim

Currency: Dinar

The ancient kingdom of Macedonia expanded during the reign of Philip II (359-336 BC), then became part of the Byzantine Empire before being conquered by the Ottoman Turks in the 14th century.

In 1913 Macedonia was divided between Serbia, Greece and Bulgaria, the Serbian region joining Yugoslavia in 1918.

Shortly after gaining independence in 1992, the country adopted a flag bearing the Star of Vergina, an emblem taken from the tomb of Philip II. However the Greeks argued that the star was a Greek emblem, so in 1995 it was replaced by the stylised sun.

The Greeks, fearing an upsurge of Macedonian nationalism, objected to the use of the Star of Vergina which adorns this gold casket from Philip II's tomb in Greece.

Bulgaria

White represents a desire for peace and liberty

Red stands for the courage of spilt blood of the freedom fighters

Green symbolises freedom and agricultural wealth

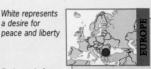

Flag ratio: 3:5

Effective date:
22 November 1990

Use: National and civil

Area: 110,912 sq. km
(42,823 sq. miles)

Capital: Sofia

Population: 8,402,000

Main language:
Bulgarian

Principal religions:
Bulgarian Orthodox,
Muslim

Currency: Lev

Bulgaria was the dominant nation in Eastern Europe until conquered by the Ottoman Turks in the late 14th century.

The country became an autonomous state in 1878 and adopted the white, green and red tricolour.

Between 1947 and 1989 Bulgaria was under dictatorial communist rule and the state emblem, featuring a rampant lion, a cog wheel and a red star, was included in the upper hoist.

Bulgarians celebrate the Festival of the Roses. The flag is adapted from the pan-Slav colours – green replacing the blue seen elsewhere in Eastern Europe.

Greece

Blue stands for the sea and sky. The shade has varied over the years

White symbolises purity

The cross represents the Greek Orthodox faith

EUROPE

Flag ratio: 2:3
Effective date: 22 December 1978
Use: National and civil

Area: 131,957 sq. km (50,949 sq. miles)
Capital: Athens
Population: 10,458,000
Main language: Greek
Principal religion: Greek Orthodox
Currency: Drachma

Greece became part of the Ottoman Empire in the 15th century and remained under Turkish rule for almost 400 years, gaining independence in 1830.

According to tradition a simple blue flag with a white cross was first hoisted by Bishop Germanos in 1821 and the striped flag was introduced the following year.

Since then the country has used both flags. From 1970 to 1974, while the Colonels were in power, only the striped flag was used, and between 1975 and 1978 the plain cross was the sole flag. In 1978 Greece readopted the striped flag, although the plain cross is still used unofficially.

The stripes of the flag stand for the nine syllables of the nationalist motto Eleutheria a thanatos, 'Freedom or Death'.

163

Romania

Nowadays the colours are said to stand for Moldavia, Transylvania and Wallachia

Flag ratio: 2:3
Effective date:
27 December 1989
Use: National and civil

Area: 238,391 sq. km (92,043 sq. miles)
Capital: Bucharest
Population: 22,680,000
Main languages: Romanian, Hungarian, German
Principal religion: Romanian Orthodox
Currency: Lev

The colours of the Romanian flag date from 1848 when the Ottoman provinces of Moldavia and Wallachia united in an attempt to free themselves from Turkish rule. Red represented Moldavia while blue stood for Oltenia (east Wallachia) and yellow for Muntenia (west Wallachia). In 1859 the provinces elected a common prince and the country was named Romania in 1862.

The colours were arranged horizontally until 1866 when, inspired by the French flag, Romania adopted the vertical tricolour. The country became a communist state in 1947 and the following year a communist emblem was added to the flag. This was removed when the Ceausescu regime was overthrown in 1989.

During the struggle to free the country from the repressive Ceausescu dictatorship the communist emblem was cut out of the flag, leaving a hole.

Moldova

The bison's head, star, rose and crescent are traditional symbols of Moldavia

The colours are based on the Romanian flag

Flag ratio: 1:2

Effective date: 3 November 1990

Use: National and civil

Area: 33,700 sq. km (13,000 sq. miles)

Capital: Kishinev

Population: 4,473,000

Main languages: Moldovan, Russian

Principal religion: Eastern Orthodox

Currency: Lev

Formerly part of the Ottoman Empire, the region of Moldavia is divided by the river Prut. The area to the west is part of Romania, while the land to the east was united with Romania before becoming the Moldavian Republic of the USSR in the 1940s.

The republic changed its name to Moldova following the collapse of the Soviet Union in 1991.

The flag adopted on independence, which bears the national arms, reflects the country's historical and cultural links with Romania.

The regions of Bukovina and Bessarabia were united by the prince of Moldavia in the 14th century to form an independent principality.

Belarus

*The distinctive pattern in the hoist
is designed to look like woven cloth*

Flag ratio: 1:2

Effective date:
7 June 1995

Use: National and civil

Area: 207,600 sq. km
(80,200 sq. miles)

Capital: Minsk

Population:
10,141,000

Main languages:
Belarussian, Russian

Principal religion:
Orthodox Christian,
Roman Catholic

Currency: Rouble

Belarus, formerly known as White Russia and Belorussia, became part of Russia in the late 18th century. In 1918 a Belorussian democratic republic was declared, however this was quickly crushed and the country became a Soviet republic the following year.

During its brief period of independence Belorussia adopted a white-red-white horizontal triband. When the republic gained independence from the USSR in 1991 the triband was restored.

In a referendum held in 1995, the majority supported closer ties with Russia and a return to the Soviet-era flag which was similar to the current design.

*The flag of Belarus flies
alongside the pan-Slav tricolour
of the Russian Federation on this
postage stamp, issued in 1996.*

Ukraine

The national colours are taken from the Ruthenian arms of 1848

Flag ratio: 2:3

Effective date:
28 January 1992

Use: National and civil

Area: 603,700 sq. km
(233,100 sq. miles)

Capital: Kiev

Population:
51,639,000

Main languages:
Ukrainian, Russian

Principal religions:
Orthodox Christian,
Ukrainian Catholic,
Muslim

Currency: Hrgvna

Formerly occupied by Russia and Austria-Hungary, Ukraine enjoyed a brief period of independence between 1918-21. The new Ukrainian National Republic adopted a flag of yellow over light blue and a few months later the colours were reversed following a coup.

Ukraine was occupied by Soviet forces in 1921 and later became part of the USSR. The flag disappeared, surfacing only occasionally as an act of protest until independence was declared in 1991 and the bicolour was readopted.

The blue and yellow bicolour represents the blue sky above the vast corn fields of the steppes.

Russian Federation

White, blue and red became known as the pan-Slavic colours, influencing many other Eastern European flags

White, blue and red are also the colours of the arms of the Duchy of Moscow

Flag ratio: 2:3

Effective date:
11 December 1993

Use: National and civil

Area:
17,075,400 sq. km
(6,592,800 sq. miles)

Capital: Moscow

Population:
147,855,000

Main languages:
Russian, Ukrainian,
Belorussian, Uzbek,
Armenian, Azerbaijani,
Georgian, many others

Principal religion:
Russian Orthodox

Currency: Rouble

Once part of the Russian Empire, the Russian Federation is the largest of the former constituent republics of the USSR.

The flag of the Federation dates back to the early 18th century when Peter the Great returned from a visit to the Netherlands where he was studying ship-building techniques. Inspired by the Dutch tricolour he adopted a similar flag for use at sea and in 1883 the flag was used on land.

The tricolour was suppressed while Russia was part of the USSR but was revived on the dissolution of the Soviet Union in 1991.

Muscovites celebrate the failure of the Soviet coup in 1991.

Russian Federation – Republic flags

 Adygeâ
(Adygeia)

Based on a design created in the 1830s by Scot, David Urquhart, the stars represent Adygeia's twelve tribes and the arrows stand for peace. The colours symbolise Islam, agriculture and freedom from oppression.

 Bashkortostan
(Bashkiria)

The flower in the centre of the flag is the Bashkor rose, unique to the region, and its petals recall the republic's seven tribes. Blue stands for virtue, white for honesty and green for eternal life and liberty.

 Burâtiâ

The flag of this Siberian republic bears the Buddhist soyonbo emblem, similar to that seen on the flag of nearby Mongolia. The colours represent water and the sky, purity, freedom and wealth.

 Chechenia

Although now officially part of the Russian Federation, Chechenia was a self-proclaimed independent state and several versions of the flag, with and without the circular emblem, are in use by various separatist groups.

 Chuvashia

The flag bears the tree of life taken from the coat of arms. Above the tree are three eight-pointed suns. The sun emblem is an ancient symbol, which also appears in the flags of Marii-Êl, Udmurtiâ and Mordoviâ.

 Dagestan

This flag, first adopted in 1992, went out of use in June 1993 and was restored in February 1994. Green represents hope and agriculture, blue stands for the Caspian Sea and red symbolises courage.

Russian Federation – Republic flags

 Gorno-Altai

The blue bands of the flag represents the republic's sky, rivers, lakes and mountains. The white field symbolises eternity and harmony.

 Ingushetiâ

This region was previously merged with Chechenia. The green bands stand for Islam and the fertile land while the emblem represents peace.

 Kabardino-Balkariâ

The central emblem depicts the Elbrus mountain, the highest peak in Europe. The flag's colours represent the sky, the snow and the prairies.

 Kalmykia

The golden yellow field of the flag and the lotus flower emblem reflect the Buddhist faith of the Mongol people of Kalmykia.

 Karachay-Cherkessia

The emblem in the centre of the flag shows the Caucasus Mountains. Blue stands for peace, green is for fertility and red represents unity and warmth.

 Kareliâ

Karelia adopted this tricolour in 1993. Blue and green recall the region's lakes and forests, while red stands for warmth and unity.

 Komi

The people of Komi are of Finnish descent. This tricolour, adopted in 1992, recalls the republic's northern landscape of snow and forests.

 Marii-Êl

The name Marii-Êl appears below the emblem, which represents the sun. The blue, white and red bands recall the pan-Slav tricolour of Russia.

Russian Federation – Republic flags

 Mordoviâ

The colours of the flag are based on the pan-Slav tricolour adopted by Russia. The traditional eight-pointed sun emblem appears in the centre.

 Qakasiâ (Khakassia)

The horizontal bands are derived from the Russian tricolour. The green stripe stands for eternal life and bears an emblem from the arms.

 Sakha

The flag depicts the sun shining in the blue sky. The white band represents snow, red symbolises flowers and courage, while green recalls the forests.

 Severnaâ Osetiâ (N. Ossetia)

Ossetia was divided in the 1920s and the south is now in Georgia. The tricolour represents agriculture and courage in the quest for freedom.

 Tatarstan

Green stands for Islam, the religion of the majority of the population, while red recalls the Russian minority and white symbolises peace between them.

 Tyviniâ (Tuva)

The Y-shape recalls the confluence of the Bii-Khem and Kaa-Khem rivers. White stands for purity, gold for wealth and Buddhism and blue for courage.

 Udmurtiâ

The republic's flag bears the ancient eight-pointed sun emblem The bands of the flag are said to represent the earth, the cosmos and the sun.

Azerbaijan

Flag ratio: 1:2
Effective date:
5 February 1991
Use: National and state

Area:
7,391,000 sq. km
Capital: Baku
Population: 7,499,000
Main languages:
Azerbaijani, Russian
Principal religion:
Muslim
Currency: Manat

The emblem recalls
the flag of Turkey, a
long-standing ally

The points of the star
represent the 8 Turkic
tribes of Azerbaijan

Azerbaijan was conquered by Russia at
the beginning of the 19th century and
became an independent state in 1918
following the Russian revolution. In 1920
it was proclaimed a Soviet Socialist
Republic, regaining independence in 1991.

The flag
adopted in 1991 was similar to
that introduced in 1918. The
colours reflect the Azerbaijani
motto 'Turkify, Islamisize and
Europeanize': light blue is a
traditional colour of the Turkic
peoples, green represents their
Islamic faith and red stands for
modernisation and progress.

*An Azerbaijani man sits at the door
of the mosque. The flag's crescent
and star emblem represents Islam,
the country's predominant religion.*

Armenia

Blue represents the sky and hope

Orange symbolises agriculture

Red stands for bloodshed

ASIA

Flag ratio: 1:2

Effective date: 24 August 1990

Use: National and state

Area: 29,800 sq. km (11,500 sq. miles)

Capital: Yerevan

Population: 3,762,000

Main languages: Armenian, Russian

Principal religion: Armenian Orthodox

Currency: Dram

For many years Armenia was a battleground for Turkish, Iranian and Russian armies.

In 1918 the Armenians established an autonomous republic and first adopted the red-blue-orange tricolour.

Armenia joined the USSR in 1922, however the flag was kept alive in exile and reinstated when the country became a unitary state in 1991.

These traditional Armenian costumes reflect the colours of the national flag.

Turkey

The star, which was added to the flag in 1793, initially had more than 5 points

The star may represent the Morning Star mentioned in the Koran

ASIA

Flag ratio: 2:3
Effective date:
5 June 1936
Use: National and civil

Area: 774,815 sq. km
(299,158 sq. miles)
Capital: Ankara
Population:
62,154,000
Main languages:
Turkish, Kurdish, Arabic
Principal religion:
Muslim
Currency: Turkish Lira

The area now known as Turkey was conquered by the Ottomans in 1453. Red flags were used by the Ottomans and the crescent emblem first appeared in the 16th century. It is said that Osman, founder of the Ottoman dynasty, dreamed of a crescent moon illuminating the world and, assuming this to be auspicious, adopted the crescent as his symbol.

According to another legend, the crescent became the emblem of Byzantium (now Istanbul) in 339BC when Philip of Macedonia's attempt to seize the city by night was detected by the light of the crescent moon.

The red flag represents Islam and the Ottoman Empire. The crescent and star have become pan-Islamic symbols.

Georgia

Black recalls the country's tragic past

White reflects the Georgians' hopes for the future

Dark red is the national colour and is said to represent happiness

ASIA

Flag ratio: 3:5

Effective date: 14 November 1990

Use: National and civil

Area: 69,700 sq. km (26,900 sq. miles)

Capital: Tbilisi

Population: 5,457,000

Main languages: Georgian, Russian

Principal religion: Georgian Orthodox

Currency: Lari

Georgia was incorporated into the Russian Empire in 1801, gaining independence in 1918 following the Russian Revolution. The state's dark red flag, which is in use again today, was originally adopted in 1917.

The country was occupied by Soviet troops in 1921, becoming part of the USSR the following year. As a Soviet republic Georgia flew a red flag with the hammer and sickle emblem in the upper hoist.

The original flag was restored on the dissolution of the Soviet Union in 1991.

The Georgian flag, shown on this stamp issued in 1992, was the winning entry in a competition held in 1917.

175

Lebanon

Red is said to stand for bloodshed

White represents peace, holiness and eternity

ASIA

Flag ratio: 2:3
Effective date:
9 December 1943
Use: National

Area: 10,400 sq. km
(4,015 sq. miles)
Capital: Beirut
Population: 3,009,000
Main languages:
Arabic, French, English
Principal religions:
Shi'a Muslim, Christian
Currency:
Lebanese pound

Formerly part of the Ottoman Empire, in 1920 Lebanon became an independent state which was administered by France until 1943. Under French mandate Lebanon used the French *tricolore* with a cedar tree in the centre. The tree had been a Lebanese symbol since Biblical times, and a white flag bearing a cedar was introduced by Maronite Christians in 1861.

In 1943 Lebanon adopted the current flag, which according to law should be red, white and green, although the tree is often seen with the trunk and branches coloured brown.

The cedar tree recalls the Bible reference: 'The righteous flourish like the palm tree, and grow like a cedar in Lebanon'.

Syria

The stars are said to represent Syria and Iraq

Red, white, black and green are the pan-Arab colours

Flag ratio: 2:3

Effective date: 29 March 1980

Use: National and civil

Area: 185,180 sq. km (71,500 sq. miles)

Capital: Damascus

Population: 14,315,000

Main languages: Arabic, Kurdish, Armenian

Principal religion: Sunni Muslim

Currency: Syrian pound

Syria came under French mandate at the end of World War I and adopted a green-white-green triband with the French *tricolore* in the canton. In 1932 nationalist sentiment led to the introduction of a green, white and black tricolour.

The red, white and black flag was first used in 1958, when Syria joined the United Arab Republic. In 1961 the previous tricolour was restored then, in 1963, the UAR flag was readopted, bearing three stars. The hawk of Quraish was substituted in 1971, signifying membership of the Federation of Arab Republics and this was later replaced by two stars.

Pan-Arab banners and portraits of president, Hafiz Al-Hassad, adorn the streets of Aleppo.

Cyprus

Flag ratio: 3:5

Effective date: circa September 1960

Use: National and civil

Area: 9,251 sq. km (3,572 sq. miles)

Capital: Nicosia

Population: 730,000

Main languages: Greek, Turkish, English

Principal religions: Greek Orthodox, Muslim

Currency: Cyprus pound

Although often coloured yellow, the island is intended to be copper reflecting the country's name, 'Copper Island'

Cyprus came under British administration in 1878 after 300 years of Turkish rule. Following an intensive terrorist campaign by Greek Cypriots seeking union with Greece, Britain granted the island independence in 1960.

The republic deliberately chose a flag of neutral design and colour to satisfy both the Greek and Turkish communities. The white field and olive branches are intended to signify peace between the two peoples. Sadly this has not been achieved and since 1974 the northern third of the island has been proclaimed an autonomous Turkish republic.

The Cypriot flag is only used internationally since the Greek and Turkish flags are flown in their respective sectors. The flag of Turkish Cyprus is white bearing a red crescent and star.

Israel

Blue and white are traditional Jewish colours

The Star of David is a centuries-old symbol of Judaism

ASIA

Flag ratio: 8:11
Effective date: 21 November 1948
Use: National

Area: 21,056 sq. km (8,130 sq. miles)
Capital: Jerusalem
Population: 5,545,000
Main languages: Hebrew, Arabic
Principal religions: Jewish, Muslim
Currency: Shekel

The goal of the Zionist movement, founded in 1897 by Theodor Herzl, was defined as the creation 'for the Jewish people of a home in Palestine secured by public law'. In 1922 Palestine came under British mandate and large-scale Jewish immigration and development began, amid violent Arab opposition.

The state of Israel was established in 1948 and adopted a flag similar to that of the Zionist movement, bearing the *Magen David* (Shield or Star of David), an ancient Jewish emblem. The flag is blue and white, based on the most common colours of the *tallit*, or prayer shawl.

The Israeli flag flies at this military base. An uneasy truce exists between Israel and its Arab neighbours.

Jordan

Red, black, white and green became the pan-Arab colours

The points of the star represent the first 7 verses of the Koran

ASIA

Flag ratio: 1:2

Effective date:
16 April 1928

Use: National and civil

Area: 97,740 sq. km
(37,738 sq. miles)

Capital: Amman

Population: 5,439,000

Main languages:
Arabic, English, French

Principal religion:
Muslim

Currency:
Jordanian dinar

From 1517 to 1918 the territory constituting Jordan was ruled by the Ottoman Turks.

Red, black, white and green were the colours of Hussein ibn Ali – king of the Hejaz (now part of Saudi Arabia), who inspired the fight for liberation – and were adopted by Jordan in 1917.

Mandated to Britain in 1920, the area east of the river Jordan was designated Transjordan. In 1946 the country was recognised as an independent kingdom and was renamed Jordan three years later.

Demonstrators struggle with a huge flag. The pan-Arab colours were later adopted by other Arab states.

Saudi Arabia

The Prophet Muhammad is said to have used a green banner

Past variants of the flag show two crossed swords

The flag is reputed to have been designed by ibn Saud's grandfather

Flag ratio: 2:3

Effective date: 15 March 1973

Use: National and civil

Area: 2,149,690 sq. km (830,000 sq. miles)

Capital: Riyadh

Population: 17,880,000

Main languages: Arabic, English

Principal religion: Sunni Muslim

Currency: Saudi riyal

The territories making up Saudi Arabia, birthplace of the prophet Muhammad, were united by Abdul Aziz ibn Saud between 1902 and 1926. Ibn Saud, leader of the Islamic Wahhabi movement, renamed the country Saudi Arabia in 1932, proclaiming himself king.

The kingdom's green flag was based on that of the Wahhabi sect. The sword of ibn Saud, given to him by his father, was added in 1902 when he became king of the Nejd (now part of Saudi Arabia).

When Saudi Arabia was established in 1932 the Nejdi flag was adopted. It bears the Muslim profession of faith, which reads: 'There is no God but Allah, and Muhammad is his Prophet'.

Saudis and Kuwaitis unite to celebrate the end of the Gulf War. Following years of dispute the Nejdi-Kuwaiti border was agreed in 1966.

Yemen

The red, white and black tricolour formed the basis of the flags of both North and South Yemen

Flag ratio: 2:3

Effective date: 22 May 1990

Use: National and civil

Area: 527,968 sq. km (203,850 sq. miles)

Capital: Sana'a

Population: 14,401,000

Main language: Arabic

Principal religion: Sunni Muslim

Currency: Riyal

In 1962 Yemen was divided forming the republics of North and South Yemen.

North Yemen became the Yemen Arab Republic and adopted a flag based on that of the United Arab Republic, with a single green star in the middle of the red, white and black tricolour.

South Yemen became the People's Democratic Republic of Yemen and flew a red, white and black flag with a blue triangle bearing a red star at the hoist.

North and South Yemen reunited in 1990 forming the Republic of Yemen and adopted a horizontal tricolour in red, white and black, the pan-Arab colours.

Tensions between North and South Yemen led to a short war in 1979.

Oman

ASIA

Flag ratio: 1:2
Effective date:
18 November 1995
Use: National and civil

Area: 212,450 sq. km
(82,030 sq. miles)
Capital: Muscat
Population: 2,163,000
Main language: Arabic
Principal religion:
Ibadi Muslim
Currency: Rial Omani

Red recalls the previous flag of the Kharijite muslims

The central band was widened in 1995

Oman, previously called Muscat and Oman, is an absolute monarchy, ruled by Sultan Qaboos bin Said who overthrew his father in a palace coup in 1970.

The new ruler renamed the country Oman and introduced a new flag. The Sultanate had previously flown the traditional plain red banner of the Kharijite muslims. In 1970 white and green panels were added, together with the state emblem of crossed scimitars and a curved *gambia* or dagger.

White stands for peace and the authority of the Imam, while green symbolises the Green Mountain range and represents Islam.

The national emblem dates from the 18th century.

United Arab Emirates

Green is a symbol of fertility

White represents neutrality

Red recalls the former flags of the Kharijite muslims

Black reflects the Emirates' oil wealth

ASIA

Flag ratio: 1:2
Effective date:
2 December 1971
Use: National and civil

Area: 83,600 sq. km
(32,278 sq. miles)
Capital: Abu Dhabi
Population: 2,314,000
Main languages:
English, Arabic,
several others
Principal religion:
Sunni Muslim
Currency: UAE dirham

The United Arab Emirates is composed of seven sheikhdoms around the Persian Gulf. The area was formerly called the Pirate Coast since pirate ships were common.

To protect its vessels, in 1853 Britain entered into the Perpetual Maritime Truce with Arab leaders and the region became known as the Trucial States. Plain red flags were traditionally flown in the Gulf states as well as by pirates, so in accordance with the truce, a white band was added to the States' flags to distinguish their vessels from pirate ships.

The current flag was adopted when the Federation was founded in 1971.

Jockeys wear the pan-Arab colours, adopted when the UAE was formed.

Qatar

ASIA

The flags of Qatar and Bahrain are very similar, reflecting the countries' historical links

The proportions of the Qatari flag are unique

Flag ratio: 11:28

Effective date: circa 1949

Use: National and civil

Area: 11,000 sq. km (4,250 sq. miles)

Capital: Doha

Population: 551,000

Main languages: Arabic, English

Principal religion: Sunni Muslim

Currency: Qatar riyal

Qatar, formerly controlled by Bahrain, then by the Ottoman Turks before becoming a British protectorate in 1916, proclaimed independence in 1971.

The sheikhdom flew the traditional plain red flag of the Kharijite Muslims until, in 1820, the British requested that friendly Gulf states add white to their flags to avoid being mistaken for pirates.

A white band was added to the flag of Qatar around 1866. In 1949 the red was officially changed to maroon, a colour which is said to have resulted from the effect of the desert sun on the local red vegetable dye.

This stamp, issued in 1996, celebrates the 25th anniversary of independence.

Bahrain

White was added to the flag to identify Bahrain as a friendly state

Red was the traditional colour of the Kharijite Sect

ASIA

Flag ratio: 3:5
Effective date:
19 August 1972

Use: National and civil

Area: 695 sq. km
(268 sq. miles)

Capital: Manama

Population: 586,000

Main languages: Arabic,
English, Farsi, Urdu

Principal religions:
Muslim

Currency:
Bahraini dinar

In the early 19th century the traditional red flag of the Kharijite Muslims – as formerly flown in Bahrain – was often used by pirate ships, so in 1820 the British asked friendly Arab states to include white in their flags to avoid confusion with pirate vessels.

Bahrain initially added a plain white band to the red flag. The serration was introduced in 1932 to distinguish the flag from that of Dubai.

Bahrain's flag is very similar to that of Qatar, differing only in the ratio and shade of red.

The Grand Mosque, Bahrain. Islam is the predominant religion recalled by the red field of the flag.

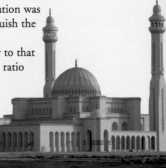

Kuwait

The flag uses the pan-Arab colours

The design may have been inspired by the pre-1958 Iraqi flag

Flag ratio: 1:2
Effective date:
24 November 1961
Use: National and civil

Area: 17,818 sq. km
(6,880 sq. miles)
Capital: Kuwait City
Population: 1,691,000
Main languages:
Arabic, English
Principal religion:
Muslim
Currency: Kuwaiti dinar

A British protectorate from 1899, Kuwait became independent in 1961 and adopted the current flag, a green, white and red horizontal tricolour with a black trapezium in the hoist.

The colours have been interpreted in different ways: black may represent the Abbasids, descendants of Muhammad's uncle Abbas, or stand for the fate of the country's enemies. Green may represent the Fatamids, who claim descent from Muhammad's daughter Fatima, or stand for agriculture. White may represent the Umayyad dynasty of Spain or stand for purity, while red may represent the Hashemite dynasty, by tradition descended from Muhammad, or the blood of the enemy.

Iraq, a former ally and possibly the source of the Kuwaiti flag, invaded the country in 1990 resulting in the Gulf War.

187

Iraq

ASIA

Red stands for courage

White represents generosity

Black symbolises Islamic triumphs

Flag ratio: 2:3

Effective date: 22 January 1991

Use: National and civil

Area: 438,317 sq. km (169,235 sq. miles)

Capital: Baghdad

Population: 20,449,000

Main languages: Arabic, Kurdish

Principal religion: Shi'a Muslim

Currency: Iraqi dinar

Iraq, which came under British mandate following World War I, was established as a kingdom under Faisal I in 1921, becoming an independent state in 1932. In 1958 the government was overthrown by a leftist coup and the country became a republic, forming a close relationship with the United Arab Republic.

The flags of Iraq have all been based on the pan-Arab colours first used by Hussein ibn Ali, king of the Hejaz and father of King Faisal. The current design, adopted in 1963, is similar to the flag of the UAR. The three stars represent Iraq and former UAR members, Syria and Egypt, expressing Iraq's desire for political union between the three counties.

Iraqi President, Saddam Hussein, ordered the invasion of Kuwait in 1990. During the ensuing Gulf War, the phrase Allahu Akbar *(God is great) was added to the flag.*

Iran

Green represents Islam

The Iranian colours date from the 18th century

Red stands for courage

White symbolises peace

ASIA

Flag ratio: 4:7

Effective date: 29 July 1980

Use: National and civil

Area: 1,633,188 sq. km (630,577 sq. miles)

Capital: Tehran

Population: 67,283,000

Main languages: Persian, Turkish, Kurdish, Luri

Principal religion: Shi'a Muslim

Currency: Rial

Iran, formerly known as Persia, was a monarchy until 1979, when the shah was toppled and exiled religious leader Ayatollah Khomeini returned to preside over the new republic.

The Islamic republic's flag bears a stylised emblem consisting of four crescents and a sword. The crescents represent Allah and bear a resemblance to the word in Arabic script. The *tashdid* above the sword is used in Arabic to double a letter, thus doubling the strength of the sword.

The inscription Allahu Akbar *is repeated 22 times along the flag's green and red bands recalling the return of Ayatollah Khomeini on the 22nd day of the Islamic month of Balman.*

Turkmenistan

The crescent symbolises Islam

The stars represent the five regions of Turkmenistan

ASIA

Flag ratio: 1:2

Effective date: 19 February 1997

Use: National and civil

Area: 488,100 sq. km (188,460 sq. miles)

Capital: Ashkhabad

Population: 4,099,000

Main languages: Turkmenian, Russian, Uzbek

Principal religion: Muslim

Currency: Manat

Turkmenistan became part of Russian Turkistan in 1881 and a republic of the USSR in 1925, declaring independence when the Soviet Union disbanded in 1991.

The following year Turkmenistan adopted a complex national flag. The field is Islamic green with a dark red band in the hoist, illustrating the traditional carpet designs, or *guls*, of the five Turkmen tribes.

The flag recalls Turkmenistan's famous carpets.

In 1997 President Niyazov decreed that an olive wreath, similar to that of the United Nations' flag, should be added below the *guls* to reflect the peace-loving Turkmen people and the country's resolution to remain permanently neutral.

Uzbekistan

Blue stands for the night sky and for water as a source of life

White represents peace

Red indicates the life-force

Green recalls nature and fertility

ASIA

Flag ratio: 1:2

Effective date: 11 October 1991

Use: National and civil

Area: 447,400 sq. km (172,750 sq. miles)

Capital: Tashkent

Population: 22,843,000

Main languages: Uzbek, Russian

Principal religion: Muslim

Currency: Sum

Uzbekistan was conquered by the Russians in the 19th century and became a republic of the Soviet Union in 1925, declaring independence in 1991.

The post-communist flag consists of blue, white and green horizontal bands separated by thin red stripes. A crescent moon and twelve stars appear in the upper hoist. The stars have been interpreted as standing for the lunar months of the Islamic calender or for the signs of the Zodiac.

The new flag has been painted on this hoarding. Although the crescent is normally an Islamic symbol, in this case it is said to represent the rebirth of the nation rather than the predominant religion.

Kazakhstan

Blue represents
the sky

The golden sun symbolises the
country's hopes for the future

Flag ratio: 1:2
Effective date:
4 June 1992
Use: National and Civil

Area:
2,717,300 sq. km
(1,049,200 sq. miles)

Capital: Astana

Population:
16,590,000

Main languages:
Kazakh, Russian

Principal religions:
Sunni Muslim,
Russian Orthodox

Currency: Tenge

The central Asian region gradually came under Russian rule between 1730 and 1853. Kazakhstan became a constituent republic of the USSR in 1936 and flew the soviet red flag with a light blue horizontal stripe. The republic declared independence when the Soviet Union dissolved in 1991.

The post-independence flag has a light blue field. In the centre of the flag an eagle, flies beneath a golden radiant sun. A band of 'national ornamentation' runs vertically at the hoist, reminiscent of the flags of Belarus and Turkmenistan.

A stone eagle surveys a deserted road beneath the blue Asian sky. The flag's emblem depicts a berkut, or steppe eagle.

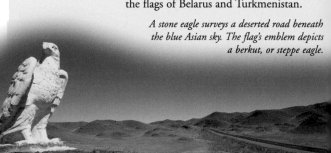

Mongolia

Red represents progress

Blue is Mongolia's national colour

Flag ratio: 1:2
Effective date: 12 February 1992
Use: National

Area: 1,565,000 sq. km (604,250 sq. miles)
Capital: Ulan Bator
Population: 2,430,000
Main language: Mongolian
Principal religions. Buddhist, atheist majority
Currency: Tugrik

Formerly a province of China, Mongolia declared independence after the Chinese revolution of 1911 and the communist People's Republic of Mongolia was founded in 1924.

The Republic adopted a red flag bearing a blue *soyonbo*, a 17th century Buddhist emblem. The Yin-Yang symbol indicates vigilance, while the flame represents progress and the triangles are a warning to enemies. The sun and moon stand for eternal life and the bars symbolise honesty and strength. In 1940 this was replaced by the current flag.

Celebrating National Day in Ulan Bator.

Kyrgyzstan

Red recalls the banner of Manas who united the Kyrgyz tribes

The emblem shows a bird's-eye view of a yurt, secured by a lattice of ropes.

ASIA

Flag ratio: 3:5
Effective date: 3 March 1992
Use: National and civil

Area: 198,500 sq. km (76,600 sq. miles)
Capital: Bishkek
Population: 4,698,000
Main languages: Kirghiz, Russian
Principal religion: Muslim
Currency: Som

The territory now known as Kyrgyzstan was annexed by Russia in 1864. In 1924 it became the autonomous region of Kara-Kirghiz joining the USSR as the Kirghiz republic in 1936. The name Kyrgyzstan was adopted in 1990 and independence was declared the following year.

The post-communist flag bears a central emblem showing a stylised yurt, viewed from above, within a golden sun. The rays of the sun represent the 40 tribes which were united by national hero, Manas, to form the Kyrgyz nation.

The yurt is the traditional felt tent of the Kyrgyz nomads.

Tajikistan

Red recalls the previous flag

Green represents agricultural produce

Flag ratio: 1:2
Effective date: 24 November 1992
Use: National and civil

Area: 143,100 sq. km (55,250 sq. miles)
Capital: Dushanbe
Population: 5,836,000
Main languages: Tajik, Uzbek, Russian
Principal religion: Sunni Muslim
Currency: Tajik rouble

Tajikistan was incorporated into the USSR in 1921, gaining independence when the Soviet Union disbanded in 1991.

As a Soviet republic Tajikistan flew a red flag with two horizontal stripes of white and green, and it was one of the last states to adopt a post-communist flag.

The current flag retains the Soviet colours, now arranged as a tricolour, reflecting the country's need for Russian support in the civil war against anti-government guerrillas.

The emblem shows a gold crown within an arc of seven stars representing sovereignty, friendship between all nationalities, and the union of workers, peasants and the intellectual classes.

Cotton is Tajikistan's chief crop, represented by the white band of the flag.

Afghanistan

Green denotes Islam

Black represents the dark past

Wheat symbolises the country's communist heritage

The Islamic year 1371 (1992), marks the date of the foundation of the new regime

Flag ratio: 1:2

Effective date:
3 December 1992

Use: National

Area: 652,090 sq. km
(251,773 sq. miles)

Capital: Kabul

Population:
20,141,000

Main languages:
Pushtu, Dari Persian

Principal religion:
Sunni Muslim

Currency: Afghani

A former monarchy, Afghanistan became a republic following a coup in 1973.

The nation's flag has changed more often than any other during its turbulent history – there have been 12 different designs so far this century.

The current tricolour, recognised by the UN, bears an Islamic emblem: a mosque enclosed within a wreath of wheat ears. Above is the *Shahada*, the Muslim profession of faith, and below is the slogan *Allahu Akbar* – 'God is Great'.

If the Taliban forces, who assumed power in Kabul in 1996, are acknowledged as the legitimate administration the flag could be revised yet again.

The white Taliban flag can now be seen at Afghan border posts.

Pakistan

Green represents Islam

The combination of green and white symbolises peace and prosperity

ASIA

Flag ratio: 2:3
Effective date:
14 August 1947
Use: National

Area: 796,095 sq. km
(307,374 sq. miles)
Capital: Islamabad
Population:
129,808,000
Main languages: Urdu,
English, Punjabi, Sindi,
Pushtu, Balochi, Brahvi
Principal religion:
Sunni Muslim
Currency:
Pakistan rupee

As part of the Indian subcontinent Pakistan was ruled by Britain from 1756. Independence was achieved in 1947 when the British withdrew following a campaign by the Muslim League, which had been formed in 1906 to represent the Islamic population.

The flag adopted on independence was based on that of the Muslim League, which was green with a white crescent and star. A vertical white band was added in the hoist to represent the non-Muslim minority.

Zulfikar Ali Bhutto, former president and prime minister of Pakistan, was ousted by a coup in 1977 and later executed.

Nepal

Initially the sun and moon had human faces but they were removed when the flag was updated in 1962

The flag is said to express the hope that Nepal will endure as long as the sun and the moon

The blue border symbolises peace

Flag ratio: 128:163

Effective date: 16 December 1962

Use: National and civil

Area: 147,181 sq. km (56,827 sq. miles)

Capital: Kathmandu

Population: 21,918,000

Main languages: Nepali, many indigenous languages

Principal religions: Hindu; Buddhist and Islamic minorities

Currency: Nepalese rupee

In 1846 Sir Jung Bahadur of the Rana family became prime minister of Nepal, the world's only Hindu monarchy, and began a period of domination in which the office of prime minister was hereditary and the kings were kept virtual prisoners. This system was ended in 1951 by King Tribhubana Bir Bikram.

Nepal's distinctive flag combines the triangular pennant of the monarchy, whose emblem is a horizontal crescent moon, with the pennant of the Rana family who are represented by the sun. These were joined together in the 19th century to form the flag's unique shape.

Crimson is the national colour which is also seen in the uniforms of the Nepalese army.

Bhutan

Saffron yellow symbolises the power of the monarchy

Orange-red stands for Buddhism

The wingless dragon holds jewels in its claws to represent prosperity

ASIA

Flag ratio: 2:3

Effective date: circa 1971

Use: National and civil

Area: 47,000 sq. km (18,147 sq. miles)

Capital: Thimphu

Population: 1,638,000

Main languages: Dzongkha, Gurung, Assamese

Principal religions: Buddhist, Hindu

Currency: Ngultrum

Lamiastic Buddhism was introduced to Bhutan by the Tibetans, who dominated the country between the 7th and mid-17th centuries.

The Tibetan name for the country is *Druk-yul*, meaning 'land of the dragon'. *Druk* is also the word for thunder because, according to tradition, the thunder frequently heard in this mountainous kingdom was believed to be the roaring of dragons.

The Tibetans set up a number of fortified monasteries in Bhutan. Here monks and novices clad in traditional red robes enjoy an annual Tibetan Buddhist festival.

India

Orange represents Hinduism

Green stands for Islam

White expresses hope for peace and unity between the two religious groups

Flag ratio: 2:3

Effective date: 22 July 1947

Use: National

Area: 3,287,590 sq. km (1,269,346 sq. miles)

Capital: New Delhi

Population: 935,744,000

Main languages: Hindi, English, Urdu, numerous others

Principal religions: Hindu, Muslim; Buddhist, Sikh, Christian and Jain minorities

Currency: Indian rupee

I ndia, formerly under British rule, gained independence in 1947 and adopted a flag based on the tricolour of the most influential nationalist organisation, the Indian National Congress, led by Mahatma Gandhi.

The flag of the Congress often bore a spinning wheel, symbolising Gandhi's call for greater economic self-sufficiency. This was replaced by a blue dharma chakra, based on that discovered at Sarnath on a

The flag's emblem is a chakra, or wheel of life, as seen on the roof of this Buddhist temple. It symbolises the law of Dharma or eternal change.

column placed by emperor Asoka around 250 BC to mark the spot where Buddha announced the Ahimsa to the four corners of the universe.

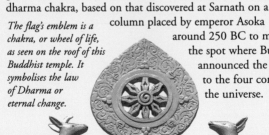

Maldives

The green panel and the crescent represent Islam

Red recalls the original flag

ASIA

Flag ratio: 2:3
Effective date:
26 July 1965
Use: National and civil

Area: 298 sq. km (115
sq. miles)
Capital: Malé
Population: 254,000
Main language: Dhivehi
Principal religion:
Sunni Muslim
Currency: Rufiyaa

Islam was introduced to the Maldives by Arab traders who arrived in the 12th century. The islands became a British protectorate in 1887, gaining independence in 1965.

Like many Muslim countries, the Maldives originally flew a plain red flag. Early this century the prime minister introduced a green panel bearing a white crescent, and a black and white diagonally striped band was later added in the hoist.

In 1949 the crescent was reversed, so the horns faced the fly, and the black and white band was dropped following independence.

Students celebrate Independence Day. The Maldives achieved autonomy as a sultanate in 1965, and the people voted to establish a republic in 1968.

201

Sri Lanka

Orange stands for the Hindu Tamils

The sword denotes authority

Green represents the Islamic minority

The four pipul leaves symbolise Buddhism

ASIA

Flag ratio: 1:2
Effective date:
7 September 1978
Use: National and civil

Area: 65,610 sq. km
(25,332 sq. miles)

Capital: Colombo

Population:
18,354,000

Main languages:
Sinhala, Tamil

Principal religions:
Buddhist, Hindu;
Christian and Islamic
minorities

Currency:
Sri Lankan rupee

A former British colony known as Ceylon, the island of Sri Lanka gained independence in 1948.

The flag adopted prior to independence bore a golden lion on a red field bordered in yellow. The green and orange panels were added in 1951 to appease the Islamic and Hindu Tamil minorities.

In 1972, when the country changed its name to Sri Lanka, four ornamental pinnacles in the corners of the red panel were replaced by leaves from the *pipul* tree, under which the Buddha sat when he received enlightenment.

The national flag was based on that of the kingdom of Kandy in the centre of the island. The leaves were modified in 1978 to make them more realistic.

Bangladesh

The red disc, set towards the hoist, recalls the fight for independence

Green represents Islam, fertility and the country's youth

Flag ratio: 3:5

Effective date:
25 January 1972

Use: National

Area: 143,998 sq. km
(55,598 sq. miles)

Capital: Dhaka

Population:
120,433,000

Main languages:
Bengali, English

Principal religions:
Muslim, Hindu

Currency: Taka

Bangladesh was ruled by Britain from the 18th century until 1947 when it became East Pakistan – 1,000 miles from West Pakistan on the other side of India.

Thousands were killed in the fight for autonomy, which resulted in a violent civil war between East and West Pakistan. Following Indian intervention East Pakistan proclaimed independence as Bangladesh in 1971.

The new national flag initially bore a gold silhouette map of the country within the red disc. This was later removed for technical reasons.

This 1971 Bangladeshi stamp celebrates the nation's victory in the struggle for autonomy.

Burma

The cog-wheel and rice plant stand for industry and agriculture

Blue symbolises peace

The stars represent the 14 states

Red denotes courage

ASIA

Flag ratio: 5:9
Effective date: 4 January 1974
Use: National and civil

Area: 676,552 sq. km (261,218 sq. miles)
Capital: Yangon (Rangoon)
Population: 44,277,000
Main languages: Burmese, Karen, Shan
Principal religions: Buddhist
Currency: Kyat

Formerly ruled by the British as part of India, Burma gained independence in 1948, adopting a flag based on that of the Anti-Fascist People's Freedom League – a wartime resistance movement which opposed the Japanese occupation of the country.

The 1948 flag was red with a blue canton containing one large white star surrounded by five small white stars.

In 1974 Burma became a Socialist Republic and a new emblem appeared in the canton, depicting a rice plant within a cog-wheel. In 1989 the country's name was officially changed to the Union of Myanmar but the existing flag was retained.

The flag adopted on independence bore six stars, representing the unity of the country's ethnic minorities.

Thailand

The central band was originally red. It was changed to blue to express solidarity with the Allies

ASIA

Flag ratio: 2:3
Effective date:
28 September 1917
Use: National and civil

Area: 513,115 sq. km
(198,115 sq. miles)
Capital: Bangkok
Population: 60,206,000
Main languages: Thai,
Chinese, Malay,
regional dialects
Principal religion:
Buddhist
Currency: Baht

Thailand, formerly Siam, was known for centuries as 'the Land of the White Elephant', recalling the legend of Zacca, founder of the nation, who was transformed into a white elephant.

The country originally flew a red flag bearing a white chakra, or Buddhist wheel. In 1817 an elephant was added in the centre and in 1855 the chakra was removed, leaving the white elephant on a red field. It is said that the king noticed a flag flying upside down, showing disrespect for the sacred emblem, so he ordered that a new flag should be designed.

The Trairanga *or tricolour flies over this new Bhuddhist temple in Phuket.*

205

Laos

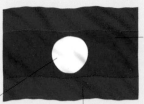

Blue stands for prosperity

White symbolises justice and the promise of the future

Red represents unity and purpose and the blood shed during the struggle for freedom

Flag ratio: 2:3

Effective date: 4 December 1975

Use: National and civil

Area: 236,800 sq. km (91,429 sq. miles)

Capital: Vientiane

Population: 4,822,000

Main languages: Lao, French, Vietnamese

Principal religions: Buddhist

Currency: Kip

In the mid-14th century the Kingdom of a Million Elephants was founded in what is now Laos. The country's original flag showed a triple-headed elephant standing on steps beneath a parasol, representing Buddhism and commemorating the Kingdom's founder, who is said to have arrived on a white elephant carrying a parasol.

This was replaced in 1975 when the Lao People's Democratic Republic was proclaimed. The new flag was based on that of the communist Pathet Lao (the Lao Patriotic Front) who took control of the country.

A parade commemorates the anniversary of the revolution. The flag introduced in 1975 is said to symbolise the full moon over the Mekong river.

Cambodia

Red and blue recall the earlier flags of Cambodia

The temple of Angkor Wat has five towers but often only three are depicted

ASIA

Flag ratio: 2:3

Effective date: 30 June 1993

Use: National and civil

Area: 181,035 sq. km (69,898 sq. miles)

Capital: Phnom Penh

Population: 9,836,000

Main languages: Khmer, French

Principal religion: Buddhist

Currency: Riel

In 1975 Cambodia came under the rule of the communist Kymer Rouge. Known as Democratic Kampuchea, the country adopted a red flag bearing a three-towered yellow silhouette of the temple at Angkor Wat. The emblem was traditional, but red represented the revolutionary new regime.

In 1979 a Vietnamese-backed puppet government was installed and the temple was modified to show all five towers. The Vietnamese withdrew in 1989 and the country was renamed the State of Cambodia.

The current flag was introduced in 1993, a few months before the monarchy was restored.

Following the Vietnamese withdrawal in 1989 a red over blue flag was adopted showing the temple in yellow with five towers.

Vietnam

Red stands for revolution and bloodshed

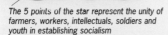

The 5 points of the star represent the unity of farmers, workers, intellectuals, soldiers and youth in establishing socialism

Flag ratio: 2:3

Effective date: 2 July 1976

Use: National and civil

Area: 331,689 sq. km (128,066 sq. miles)

Capital: Hanoi

Population: 74,545,000

Main languages: Vietnamese, French, English

Principal religion: Buddhist

Currency: Dông

Vietnam, previously under French rule, was occupied by Japan in 1940. Communist leader, Ho Chi Minh formed the Viet Minh (Independence) League and, when the Japanese surrendered in 1945, he declared independence – which the French were unwilling to concede.

In 1954 it was agreed that North Vietnam should be controlled by the communists, who adopted the Viet Minh flag – a yellow star on a red field – modifying the shape of the star.

North Vietnam sought to take over the South and civil war ensued. When South Vietnam surrendered and was reunited with the North to form the Socialist Republic of Vietnam in 1976, the flag of North Vietnam was retained.

A stand in Ho Chi Minh city sells flags and portraits of the former leader.

Malaysia

Yellow is the colour of the Sultans of Malaysia

The blue canton recalls the British Empire and represents unity

Red and white are the traditional colours of South East Asia

Flag ratio: 1:2
Effective date: 16 September 1963
Use: National and civil

Area: 329,749 sq. km (127,317 sq. miles)

Capital: Kuala Lumpur

Population: 20,140,000

Main languages: Malay, English, Chinese, Indian languages

Principal religions: Muslim, Hindu, Buddhist

Currency: Ringgit

Formerly under British rule, the Union of Malay States was formed in 1946 and later renamed the Malay Federation. In 1950 the Federation adopted a flag inspired by the Stars and Stripes, bearing eleven red and white stripes with a gold crescent and an eleven-pointed star in a blue canton, representing the member states.

In 1963, when Sabah, Sarawak and Singapore joined the Federation, the country was renamed Malaysia and the stripes were increased to 14, as were the points of the star. The flag was not changed when Singapore left in 1965. Instead the 14th stripe and point of the star were said to represent the federal territory of Kuala Lumpur.

The crescent represents Islam, practised by around 50 per cent of the population.

Malaysia – State flags

 Johore

The flag's red canton represents the Hulubalang, *the state warriors*, and white symbolises the Sultan. The blue field stands for the government.

 Kedah

The emblem consists of a green crescent, representing Islam, within a wreath of rice, the state's main crop. The shield is a symbol of the Sultan.

 Kelantan

The emblem, which consists of two spears, two torches and a crescent and star stands for the ruler. Red symbolises the loyalty of the people.

 Kuala Lumpur

The red and white stripes stand for courage and purity. The central blue band represents unity and yellow symbolises wealth and the ruler.

 Labuan

Labuan is an island off the coast of Sabah and was formerly part of North Borneo. The state's flag uses the national colours.

 Melaka

The colours signify that Melaka is a member state of the Federation of Malaysia. The star and crescent emblem represents Islam.

 Negeri Sembilan

The flag's yellow field represents the ruler, while the black triangle stands for the district chiefs and the red triangle symbolises the people.

 Pahang

The bicolour dates from the early 1900s. The upper white band represents the ruler and the black stripe below stands for the people.

Malaysia– State flags

Perak

The white band at the top represents the Sultan and his superior position. The yellow and black bands stand for junior members of the royal family.

Perlis

Yellow, the traditional colour of the ruler, is placed above the blue band, which represents the people. Both are of equal width signifying co-operation.

Pinang

The emblem is a Pinang palm, or betelnut, tree. Blue represents the sea which surrounds the island and yellow stands for prosperity.

Sabah

Mount Kinabalu appears in the canton of the flag. The blue stripe represents strength, white stands for purity and red represents courage.

Sarawak

Yellow symbolises unity, law and order, while red stands for courage and black for natural resources. The points of the star represent the nine districts.

Selangor

Yellow and red represent flesh and blood and symbolise the life of the state. The star and crescent, which were originally yellow, stand for Islam.

Terengganu

Black is for the people, surrounded by the protection of the Sultan, who is represented by white. The crescent and star stand for Islam.

Indonesia

White stands for the soul, purity and justice

Red represents the body as well as gallantry and freedom

Flag ratio: 2:3
Effective date: 17 August 1945
Use: National and civil

Area: 1,904,569 sq. km (735,358 sq. miles)

Capital: Jakarta

Population: 193,750,000

Main languages: Bahasa Indonesian, English, local languages

Principal religion: Muslim

Currency: Rupiah

The colours of the Indonesian flag are said to date back to the Javanese Majapahit Empire which dominated Indonesia and Malaya between the 13th and 16th centuries.

The Dutch took control of Java in the mid-18th century, and extended their influence until the whole of present-day Indonesia was united under Dutch rule in the early 20th century.

The red and white bicolour was revived by nationalists in the 1920s becoming the national flag when Indonesia declared

independence following World War II.

Red and white are traditional South East Asian colours. The Indonesian flag is identical to that of Monaco, except in its proportions.

Singapore

ASIA

Red represents universal fellowship and equality

White stands for purity and virtue

Red and white are traditional colours in South East Asia

Flag ratio: 2:3

Effective date:
3 December 1959

Use: National and civil

Area: 618 sq. km
(239 sq. miles)

Capital: Singapore

Population: 2,987,000

Main languages:
Mandarin, Malay, Tamil, English

Principal religions:
Buddhist, Christian, Muslim, Taoist

Currency:
Singapore dollar

Singapore was a British colony before 1963, when it joined the Federation of Malaysia, leaving two years later.

The red and white flag was adopted in 1958 when the island became a self-governing state. It was originally intended to be plain red to reflect the Chinese origins of 80 per cent of the population, but this was rejected because of red's communist connotations. Similarly the initial design bearing three stars was modified because of its resemblance to the flag of the Malayan Communist Party.

The crescent and stars have no Islamic significance – they are said to symbolise the ascent of the young nation based on democracy, peace, progress, justice and equality.

Banners celebrate Singapore's 31st National Day.

珍珠百货商坊热烈庆祝我国独立世
PEOPLE'S PARK CELEBRATES 31th NATIONAL

全民团结一

Brunei

The flag and umbrella are based on ancient royal regalia while the mast represents the state

The four-feathered wing, the Sayap symbolises the protection of justice, tranquillity, prosperity and peace

The scroll reads 'Brunei City of Peace'

Flag ratio: 1:2
Effective date: circa 1984
Use: National and civil

Area: 5,765 sq. km (2,226 sq. miles)
Capital: Bandar Seri Begawan
Population: 285,000
Main languages: Malay, English, Chinese
Principal religions: Muslim, Buddhist, Christian
Currency: Brunei dollar

The Sultanate of Brunei became a British protectorate in 1888 gaining independence in 1984. When the country came under the administration of a British resident in 1906 diagonal white and black bands were superimposed on the Sultan's plain yellow flag, implying that he no longer held absolute power.

The state emblem was added in 1959 when the country became self-governing. Upturned hands either side signify the government's pledge to promote welfare, peace and prosperity.

A mosque on Kalimantan Island, Brunei. Islam is represented by the crescent which bears the motto 'Always in service with God's guidance'.

Philippines

Blue expresses patriotism and noble ideals

Red denotes bravery

White symbolises peace and purity

The stars stand for the 3 island groups: Luzon, the Visayas and Mindanao

Flag ratio: 1:2

Effective date: 25 March 1936

Use: National and civil

Area: 300,000 sq. km (115,830 sq. miles)

Capital: Manila

Population: 70,267,000

Main languages: Filipino, English, Spanish, local languages

Principal religion: Roman Catholic

Currency: Peso

The Philippine Islands came under Spanish control in the 16th century. The struggle for independence began in the late-19th century, led by nationalist Emilio Aguinaldo, head of the Katipunan movement. The current flag was introduced by Aguinaldo in 1898 and became the national flag on independence in 1946.

A unique feature of the flag is that it is flown with blue uppermost in peacetime, and the colours are reversed in wartime.

The sun in the hoist of the flag, which appears on this postage stamp, represents the dawning of a new era and the rays refer to the eight provinces which opposed Spanish rule.

Taiwan

Known as 'white sun in blue sky,' the flag of Sun Yat-sen appears in the canton

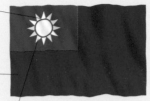

Red is a traditional Chinese colour

The rays of the sun represent 12 traditional Chinese hours (each equalling two hours) symbolising progress

Flag ratio: 2:3

Effective date: 8 October 1928

Use: National

Area: 35,742 sq. km (13,800 sq. miles)

Capital: Taipei

Population: 21,299,000

Main languages: Mandarin, Chinese, Taiwanese, Hakka dialect

Principal religions: Buddhist, Taoist, Confucianist

Currency: New Taiwan dollar

Formerly part of the Chinese Empire, Taiwan was occupied by the Japanese from 1895 until 1945 when it was returned to China. The Chinese flag was that of the ruling *Kuomintang* (Nationalist party), based on a flag adopted in 1895 by the party's founder Sun Yat-sen.

Between 1945 and 1949 the *Kuomintang* government, led by Chiang Kai-shek, was engaged in a civil war against the communists, who eventually won control of mainland China. In 1949 the *Kuomintang* fled to Taiwan, where the flag was retained.

Formerly the flag of China, the Kuomintang *flag has now been adopted by Taiwan.*

China

The large star symbolises the common programme of the Communist Party

The small stars represent the four economic classes: peasants, workers, petty bourgeoisie and 'patriotic capitalists'

ASIA

Flag ratio: 2:3
Effective date:
1 October 1949

Use: National and civil

Area:
9,596,961 sq. km
(3,705,408 sq. miles)

Capital: Beijing

Population:
1,221,462,000

Main languages:
Mandarin, Cantonese,
Yue, Wu, Hakka, Xiang,
Gan, other local
languages

Principal religions:
officially atheist,
Buddhist, Taoism

Currency:
Renminbi Yuan

When the Kuomintang came to power in 1928, China adopted the party's flag, which was red with a white sun in a blue canton. In 1949 the communists ousted the *Kuomintang*, who fled to Taiwan, where their flag is still in use.

In its place China adopted the red flag of the Communist Party. Red stands for revolution, but is also a traditional Chinese colour, recalling the dominant Han race, and representing happiness and good fortune.

A figure paints the Chinese flag over that of Macau on this T-shirt, anticipating the return of the Portuguese territory to Chinese rule in 1999.

217

North Korea

White stands for purity

Red represents communist revolution

Blue expresses the desire for peace

ASIA

Flag ratio: 1:2

Effective date: 8 September 1948

Use: National and civil

Area: 120,538 sq. km (46,540 sq. miles)

Capital: Pyongyang

Population: 23,917,000

Main language: Korean

Principal religions: almost non-existent, traditionally Buddhist, Confucianist

Currency: Won

The Kingdom of Korea was under Japanese rule from 1910 until the end of World War II, when the USSR and the United States agreed to divide the country.

The USSR occupied the area north of the 38th parallel and gave its support to North Korea's Communist party, formed in 1946 under the leadership of Kim Il Sung.

The Democratic People's Republic of Korea was founded in 1948, with Kim Il Sung as premier. The flag of the DPRK retains the colours of the flag of the Kingdom of Korea and bears a red communist star on a white disc set towards the hoist.

US troops, who occupied South Korea after World War II, lower the North Korean flag in 1951.

South Korea

This trigram symbolises summer, south and heaven

This trigram represents autumn, west and the moon

This trigram represents spring, east and the sun

This trigram stands for winter, north and the Earth

ASIA

Flag ratio: 2:3

Effective date: 21 February 1984

Use: National and civil

Area: 99,274 sq. km (38,330 sq. miles)

Capital: Seoul

Population: 44,851,000

Main language: Korean

Principal religions: Christian, Mahayana Buddhist

Currency: Won

After World War II the Kingdom of Korea, forcibly annexed by Japan in 1910, was divided and South Korea was occupied by the United States.

The Republic of Korea was established in 1948 and adopted a modified version of Korea's original flag, first used in 1882.

In the centre is a traditional yin-yang symbol representing the affinity of opposites. This is surrounded by four black trigrams from the *I Ching*, an ancient Chinese book used for divination. Each has three meanings, symbolising the seasons, the points of the compass and the elements of the universe.

South Korean fans at the 1998 Winter Olympics. White is a traditional colour expressing purity and the desire for peace.

Japan

The mon is called Hi-no-maru or sun-disc

White symbolises honesty and purity

The disc is set slightly towards the hoist

ASIA

Flag ratio: 7:10
Effective date:
5 August 1854

Use: National and civil

Area: 377,682 sq. km
(145,682 sq. miles)

Capital: Tokyo

Population:
125,197,000

Main language:
Japanese

Principal religion:
Shinto Buddhist

Currency: Yen

The red sun emblem which appears on Japan's flag reflects the Japanese name for the country, *Dai Nippon*, meaning Land of the Rising Sun, as well as the claim that its emperors are descendants of the sun goddess.

The emblem, known as the state *mon* or heraldic symbol, is said to date back to the Tokugawa family who ruled Japan for 300 years until, in 1867, the emperor was restored. The following year Emperor Mutsuhito established the *Meiji* ('enlightened') government and the flag was officially adopted.

Red noses at the 1998 Winter Olympics.

Australia

The Union Jack marks Australia's historical links with Britain

The Southern Cross helped guide early European navigators to the continent

Flag ratio: 1:2

Effective date: 15 April 1954

Use: National and civil

Area: 7,741,220 sq. km (2,988,902 sq. miles)

Capital: Canberra

Population: 18,090,000

Main languages: English, Aboriginal languages

Principal religions: Protestant, Roman Catholic

Currency: Australian dollar

In the 18th century Captain James Cook landed in Australia and claimed the country for Great Britain. While the Union Jack remained the official flag, in the early 1900s a competition was held to find a flag for the new nation. Among the thousands of entries were six remarkably similar submissions, which were combined to produce the final design. The flag was given royal assent in 1954.

Below the Union Jack is the seven-pointed 'Star of Federation' which represents the six federal states and the associated territories. The Southern Cross in the fly is a constellation visible from all the states and territories.

The Aboriginal flag, which represents Australia's original inhabitants, was hoisted in 1971. Red represents the land, black stands for the people and gold symbolises the sun, the source of life.

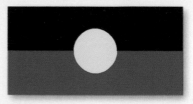

Australia – State flags

 Australia Capital Territory

The flag, adopted in 1993, is based on designs resulting from a competition. It bears the Southern Cross and the City of Canberra's coat of arms.

 New South Wales

The badge consists of a St George's cross with a golden lion in the centre and a gold star on each arm. The flag dates from 15 February 1876.

 Northern Territory

The flag uses the territory's colours: black, white and ochre. The desert rose has seven petals symbolising the six states plus the territories.

 Queensland

The emblem of Queensland is a blue Maltese cross bearing the royal crown, on a white field. The flag was adopted on 29 November 1876

 South Australia

The state bird, the white-backed piping shrike, appears on the badge. Until 1904 the state badge depicted Britannia talking to an aborigine.

 Tasmania

The emblem of the island of Tasmania is a red lion, which also appears on the crest of the state arms. The flag was adopted in 1876.

 Victoria

The Southern Cross constellation appears in the fly surmounted by a crown. The flag of Victoria is one of the oldest state flags.

 Western Australia

The badge depicts the black swan which is native to Western Australia. The flag was adopted in 1875 and the emblem was modified in 1953.

Vanuatu

Red symbolises blood

Yellow represents sunshine

Black reflects the Melanesian population

Green stands for the islands' riches

OCEANIA

Flag ratio: 3:5

Effective date: 30 July 1980

Use: National and civil

Area: 12,189 sq. km (4,706 sq. miles)

Capital: Vila

Population: 165,000

Main languages: French, English, Bislama

Principal religions: Protestant, Roman Catholic

Currency: Vatu

The New Hebrides were under joint British and French control before gaining independence as Vanuatu in 1980.

The country's new flag was designed by a local artist and the colours are those of the dominant Vanuaaku Party. The prime minister suggested that the black and yellow fimbriations should be added to accentuate the black triangle representing the islanders. The Y-shape mirrors the pattern formed by the group of islands and the crossed leaves of the namele fern signify peace.

The Vanuatu civil air ensign includes the boar's tusk, which appears on the national flag. It represents prosperity, because an islander needs status and wealth to keep a pig.

Fiji

The bright blue field stands for the Pacific Ocean

The shield is taken from the coat of arms

Flag ratio: 1:2
Effective date: 10 October 1970
Use: National and civil

Area: 18,274 sq. km (7,056 sq. miles)
Capital: Suva
Population: 796,000
Main languages: English, Fijian, Hindi
Principal religions: Roman Catholic, Methodist, Hindu, Muslim
Currency: Fiji dollar

A British colony from 1874, Fiji achieved independence in 1970. A national competition was held to find a new flag, and the design chosen is very similar to the former colonial ensign.

The Union Jack in the canton reflects Fiji's continuing economic and political links with Britain.

The shield in the fly shows a lion holding a peeled coconut, three sugar canes, a coconut palm, a dove holding an olive branch and a bunch of bananas.

Agriculture forms the basis of the Fijian economy and features strongly in the coat of arms. Coconuts are an important export crop and also appeared on the arms of the King of Fiji.

Papua New Guinea

The bird of paradise represents liberty

The Southern Cross recalls the country's links with Australia

OCEANIA

Flag ratio: 3:4
Effective date: 16 September 1975
Use: National and civil

Area: 462,840 sq. km (178, 704 sq. miles)
Capital: Port Moresby
Population: 4,074,000
Main languages: English, Melanesian and Papuan languages
Principal religions: Protestant, Roman Catholic, indigenous
Currency: Kina

Papua New Guinea comprises Papua, previously an Australian dependency, and the former German colony of New Guinea and the Solomon Islands, which were united in 1949 under Australian administration.

A national flag was adopted in 1971, and the country gained full independence in 1975.

The flag was designed by local artist, Susan Karike, using traditional colours, frequently seen in native art.

The bird of paradise is a widespread emblem, which appeared on a previous unofficial flag.

Solomon Islands

Yellow symbolises the sun

Blue stands for the Pacific ocean and water on which life depends

Green represents the lush vegetation

OCEANIA

Flag ratio: 1:2

Effective date: 18 November 1977

Use: National and civil

Area: 28,896 sq. km (11,157sq. miles)

Capital: Honiara

Population: 378,000

Main languages: English, Papuan, Melanesian, Polynesian

Principal religions: Protestant, Roman Catholic, indigenous

Currency: Soloman Island dollar

The Solomon Islands were under German control from 1885 to 1900, when the islands (except Bougainville and Buka, which are now part of Papua New Guinea) were transferred to the British. Independence was achieved in 1978, and the country's flag, adopted in 1977, was created as a result of an unofficial competition and much local debate.

The stars originally symbolised the five administrative districts, but when these were increased to seven, the stars were said to stand for the five island groups.

A Melanesian man poses in traditional native dress. The ceremonial shield is typical of the intricate work of artisans in the central Soloman Islands.

Palau

The disc is set towards the hoist

The disc represents the full moon, traditionally the most auspicious time for work and celebration

OCEANIA

Flag ratio: 5:8
Effective date: 1 January 1981
Use: National and civil

Area: 458 sq. km (177 sq. miles)
Capital: Koror
Population: 17,000
Main languages: English, Palauan, local languages
Principal religions: Christian, Modekngei
Currency: US dollar

Formerly controlled by Spain, Germany and Japan, Palau came under American administration after World War II, gaining independence in 1994. The country's flag, created as a result of a local competition, was adopted in 1980 when the islands became a self-governing republic.

The flag is said to represent the moon shining over the sea, which expresses feelings of warmth, tranquillity, peace, love and domestic harmony. However the blue field is also symbolic of the move towards autonomy.

The republic of Palau consists of over 200 of the western Caroline islands, only eight of which are inhabited.

Federated States of Micronesia

The stars represent the states of Ponape, Kosrae, Yap and Truk

The blue field is said to represent the Pacific Ocean

Flag ratio: 10:19

Effective date: 30 November 1978

Use: National and civil

Area: 702 sq. km (271 sq. miles)

Capital: Palikir

Population: 105,000

Main language: English

Principal religion: Roman Catholic

Currency: US dollar

Micronesia consists of several small islands in the western Pacific, which gained independence in 1979.

The blue flag has been in use since 1962, when it bore six stars representing Truk, Yap, Ponape, the Marshall Islands, Palau and the Northern Marianas. When the Marshall Islands and Palau became independent states the number of stars was reduced to four, arranged as the points of a compass.

The Northern Marianas left the federation, becoming a self-governing US commonwealth, and in 1977 the state of Kosrae was formed out of part of Ponape.

Micronesia was formerly part of the UN Trust Territory of the Pacific Islands, and the flag's colours are derived from those of the UN. In this ceremony both flags are hoisted alongside the Stars and Stripes.

Marshall Islands

Flag ratio: 10:19
Effective date:
1 May 1979
Use: National and civil

Area: 181 sq. km
(70 sq. miles)
Capital:
Dalap-Uliga-Darrit
Population: 54,000
Main languages:
English, Marshallese,
Japanese
Principal religion:
Protestant
Currency: US dollar

Orange stands for bravery

The blue field represents the Pacific Ocean

White symbolises peace

Formerly owned by Germany, the Marshall Islands came under Japanese control in 1914 and were captured by the Americans during World War II.

The flag adopted when the country became self-governing in 1979 was designed by the president's wife. The widening stripes – said to reflect the islands' growing development and vitality – symbolise the two chains of islands: orange stands for Ralik (Sunset) and white for Ratak (Sunrise).

The star represents the Christian cross. The extended rays symbolise the capital and the districts of Ebeye, Jaluit and Wotje; the remaining 20 points stand for the municipalities.

The Americans, who controlled the islands during World War II, used Bikini atoll as a nuclear testing ground.

Nauru

Blue stands for the Pacific Ocean

The points of the star symbolise the island's twelve original tribes

The yellow stripe represents the equator

Flag ratio: 1:2
Effective date:
31 January 1968
Use: National and civil

Area: 21 sq. km
(8.1 sq. miles)
Capital: Yaren
Population: 10,000
Main language:
Nauruan
Principal religion:
Christian
Currency:
Australian dollar

Nauru was occupied by the Japanese during World War II, after which it it was administered jointly by Australia, Britain and New Zealand before gaining independence in 1968.

The flag adopted on independence reflects the island's position one degree south of the equator. The white star, which represents Nauru, is situated towards the hoist, possibly marking the island's location to the east of the international date line, or perhaps echoing the flag of Australia.

The flag of Nauru, which appears on this 1988 postage stamp, was the winning entry in a design competition.

NAURU

100 Years in
Universal
Postal
Union
1 October 1988
$1.00

Kiribati

The waves represent the Pacific Ocean

The flag was selected following a design competition

OCEANIA

Flag ratio: 1:2

Effective date: 12 July 1979

Use: National and civil

Area: 726 sq. km (280 sq. miles)

Capital: Tarawa

Population: 78,000

Main language: English, I-Kiribati

Principal religion: Roman Catholic

Currency: Australian dollar

Kiribati (pronounced *Kiribas*) was formerly known as the Gilbert Islands. The islands were a British protectorate from 1892 and attained independence in 1979.

The national flag is a banner of the coat of arms which appeared on the Blue Ensign flown before independence. The waves and the red sky have been extended – a design unpopular with the College of Arms which chose to enlarge the sun and the frigate bird. The people of Kiribati demanded a return to the original design, however, and this was hoisted on independence.

The frigate bird, which also appears on the coat of arms, symbolises control of the sea.

Tuvalu

The Union Jack signifies the islands' wish to preserve links with Britain

The nine stars representing the islands are placed according to their locations

Flag ratio: 1:2

Effective date: 11 April 1997

Use: National and civil

Area: 26 sq. km (10 sq. miles)

Capital: Funafuti

Population: 10,000

Main languages: Tuvaluan, English

Principal religion: Protestant

Currencies: Tuvalu dollar, Australian dollar

The Ellice Islands, once part of the British protectorate known as The Gilbert and Ellice Islands Colony, separated from the Gilberts in 1975, becoming the independent state of Tuvalu in 1978. The name means 'Eight standing together', referring to the country's eight populated islands. However, the ninth is now inhabited and the nine islands are represented on the flag by nine stars.

In 1995 prime minister, Kamuta Lautasi, introduced a new flag with a complex design of stars and stripes. This outraged the local population and Mr Lautasi was deposed in 1997 by Bikenibeu Paenui, whose first act as prime minister was to restore the original flag.

The Polynesian people of Tuvalu voted for separation from the Micronesians who inhabit the Gilberts (now Kiribati).

Samoa

Red and white are traditional colours, dating back to the flag of 19th century Samoan king, Malietoa Laupepa

The Southern Cross constellation links Samoa to other countries in the southern hemisphere

OCEANIA

Flag ratio: 1:2

Effective date: 4 July 1997

Use: National and civil

Area: 2,831 sq. km (1,093 sq. miles)

Capital: Apia

Population: 171,000

Main languages: Samoan, English

Principal religion: Protestant

Currency: Tala

A former German colony, Samoa was placed under the administration of New Zealand following World War I and became an independent state in 1962.

In 1948 the country adopted a national flag, which bore four stars representing the Southern Cross, reminiscent of the flag of New Zealand.

The smaller fifth star was added the following year, making the flag more similar to those of Australia and Papua New Guinea.

US-backed King Maliatoa Tanu won succession to the Samoan throne over his German-supported opponent Mataafa.

Tonga

Red represents the blood of Christ

OCEANIA

Flag ratio: 1:2
Effective date:
circa 1862

Use: National and civil

Area: 747 sq. km
(288 sq. miles)

Capital: Nuku'alofa

Population: 98,000

Main languages:
Tongan, English

Principal religion:
Protestant

Currency: Pa'anga

Following a period of unrest and civil war, the islanders of Tonga were united by King George Tupou I in 1845. He brought Christianity to the people and, in 1862, requested a flag which would reflect his strong Christian beliefs.

The initial design was a red cross on a plain white field, however this was later found to be similar to the flag of the Red Cross, which was introduced in 1864. The design was modified, and in 1875 a red flag was adopted with the original red cross in a white canton.

The constitution of Tonga states that the flag should never be changed.

The red cross, which proclaims the islanders' Christian faith, has become Tonga's national emblem.

New Zealand

The Union Jack marks New Zealand's historical links with Britain

The stars represent the Southern Cross

OCEANIA

Flag ratio: 1:2

Effective date: 12 June 1902

Use: National and civil

Area: 270,534 sq. km (104,454 sq. miles)

Capital: Wellington

Population: 3,542,000

Main languages: English, Maori

Principal religion: Protestant, Roman Catholic

Currency: New Zealand dollar

A former British colony, New Zealand achieved independence in 1931.

The country's first flag was chosen by a group of Maori chiefs in 1834. This was white bearing the cross of St George, with a blue canton containing another cross and four white stars.

The current flag is based on the British Blue Ensign. It was designed in 1869 but its use was restricted until it was officially adopted in 1902.

A stylised version of the Southern Cross appears in the fly and only four of the usual five stars are depicted. These all vary slightly in size.

Captain James Cook visited New Zealand in 1769 and took possession of the islands on behalf of Great Britain.

International flags

 Arab League

The green field and the crescent represent Islam. The emblem shows a circular chain linking the Arab states, within a wreath of laurel leaves.

 ASEAN

The flag of the Association of South East Asian Nations depicts six sheaves of rice, representing the member states. Blue stands for the sea and the sky.

 Caricom

The colours of the flag representing the Caribbean Community and Common Market symbolise the sun, the sea and the sky.

 The Commonwealth

The emblem includes the letter 'C' made up of rays, which originally stood for the member states. A globe appears in the centre.

 CIS

The flag of the Commonwealth of Independent States (formerly soviet republics) shows a stylised tree encircling the sun against a blue sky.

 European Union

The flag adopted in 1953 bore 15 stars, representing the member states. For practical reasons as more states joined, the stars were restricted to 12.

 NATO

The flag of the North Atlantic Treaty Organization bears a circle, standing for unity, and a compass rose. Blue represents the Atlantic Ocean.

 OAS

The emblem of the Organization of American States displays the flags of the US and the Caribbean and Latin American members of the Alliance.

International flags

 OAU

The emblem of the Organization of African Unity includes a map of the continent. The colours symbolise the forests and deserts. White is for peace.

 Olympic Flag

The flag was first hoisted at the Antwerp Games in 1920. The interconnected rings represent the five continents competing in harmony.

 OPEC

The flag of the Organization of Petroleum-Exporting Countries, founded in 1960, uses the colours of the United Nations.

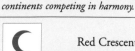 Red Crescent

As a Christian symbol, the Red Cross was considered inappropriate for use in Muslim countries, so the Red Crescent flag was created.

 Red Cross

The Red Cross flag, which originated at a conference in Geneva in 1863, is based on that of Switzerland, a country famed for its neutrality.

 South Pacific Commission

The flag's blue field represents the Pacific Ocean while the stars stand for the member states. The palm tree recalls the region's natural vegetation.

 United Nations

A symbol of peace, the olive wreath emblem and UN colours are known worldwide and have been adopted by other groups and nations.

 WEU

The flag of the Western European Union bears the Union's initials in English and French plus nine stars, which represent the member states.

Index